T0148858

PENGUIN BOOKS

THREADING WORLDS: CONVERSATIONS ON MENTAL HEALTH
WEAVING BETWEEN LIGHT AND SHADOWS,
SAID AND UNSAID

As an internationally recognised spiritual teacher, professional artist, social healer, life coach, and community leader, Hun Ming Kwang is relentless in his mission to illuminate individuals to their deepest truths, callings and authentic selves, helping them awaken and harness their power to actualize their lives at their highest creative potential. Today, he has helped over 10,000 individuals transform their lives and attain a higher level of awareness.

He also focuses on championing humanitarian campaigns and efforts to invoke and inspire awareness on social causes such as mental health and suicide prevention at a national level. He is the founder and co-artistic director of ThisConnect.today, where he designs and produces experiential art, interactive films and conscious conversations to make a difference to the public.

Threading Worlds:
Conversations on Mental Health
Weaving Between Light and Shadows, Said and Unsaid

Hun Ming Kwang

PENGUIN BOOKS

An imprint of Penguin Random House

PENGUIN BOOKS

USA | Canada | UK | Ireland | Australia
New Zealand | India | South Africa | China | Southeast Asia

Penguin Books is part of the Penguin Random House group of companies
whose addresses can be found at global.penguinrandomhouse.com

Published by Penguin Random House SEA Pvt. Ltd
9, Changi South Street 3, Level 08-01,
Singapore 486361

First published in Penguin Books by Penguin Random House SEA 2022
Copyright © Hun Ming Kwang 2022

ISBN 9789815058260

Typeset in Garamond by MAP Systems, Bengaluru, India

www.penguin.sg

Contents

Foreword

The latest Singapore Mental Health Study shows one in seven people has experienced some mental health challenges in their lifetime and more than 75 per cent of these did not seek any professional help.[1] *Threading Worlds: Conversations on Mental Health* Volumes seek to close this treatment gap.

The transcribed authentic voices of healthcare professionals and other community leaders and those with lived experiences will help us reach the self-realization of our own state of mental wellness. It will move us to co-create a safe space for the community to talk openly about the challenges and the solutions with courage and empathy.

One of the causes of the treatment gap is the stigmatization of the condition, driving us away from seeking treatment. I have been to ThisConnect's multimedia art exhibitions and one of the works—*Connection without Sight* shows us how we can connect deeply through our primal senses and emotional centres without succumbing to the superficial judgement of sight.

Active listening is essential for deep understanding with empathy without which the advice we give and receive are likely

---

[1] Subramaniam, M., E. Abdin, J. A. Vaingankar, S. Shafie, B. Y. Chua, R. Sambasivam, Y. J. Zhang, et al., "Tracking the Mental Health of a Nation: Prevalence and Correlates of Mental Disorders in the Second Singapore Mental Health Study", Epidemiology and Psychiatric Sciences 29, 2020: e29. doi:10.1017/S2045796019000179

to be irrelevant and superfluous. Another work—*I Feel You* will enable us to stand in the shoes of others and be there to hold that safe sacred space for another human being.

Masks of Singapore, a six-month local community self-awareness mask-making project, depict the façade that most people portray to one another in our daily interactions. We wear these 'masks' to suppress our true mental state. The making of masks will help us discover our true self and give ourselves permission to express our truth more freely than ever.

This project is a cool way to create a healing place for us to courageously confront our own mental health challenges in a safe space. Wherever these books are found, a safe space is created to mine the comprehensive information leading one to seek treatment. I wish Ming Kwang and his team luck and may their endeavours be perfectly accomplished.

Dr William Wan, PhD, JP.
General Secretary,
Singapore Kindness Movement

To You: A Message From the Author

Dear Reader,

If by a stroke of luck, a gesture of goodwill, something about this book resonated with you, found its way to you, and landed in your hands—let it be a sign that there are certain answers in your life that you're searching for.

Before we begin, I would like to invite you to take a moment to picture this:

You're a student in your teens or early twenties. You're spending thousands of dollars on a formal education as you work your way up to a university degree, studying subjects only for the purpose of excelling the exams, while juggling several other commitments such as an internship, a part-time job, an extra-curricular activity, to boost your credentials and show your potential employers that you have some degree of holistic development, real-world experience, and a life outside of your studies. Along the way, you might have countless nights of overwhelming stress, pressure, burnout, and negative downward spirals. You ask yourself endlessly—are you disappointing your family? Are you failing the expectations that others have of you? Are you on track to landing a stable job once you graduate? Do you have enough commitments on your plate to ensure you're not any less ambitious than your peers? Your teachers might have good intentions, but the most they tell you is 'Don't stress too much, just remain calm, be positive, be happy, and do your best'—as if those things never automatically occurred to you before. In a world full of adults who appear to have figured out all the answers to life, are you a failure if you can't be positive and calm without distracting yourself and numbing away your anger, sadness, and negativity?

This might also be the period where you struggle to make sense and find your place in your social world. How do people view you? Who are the friends who are going to stick by you as you enter adulthood and into the working world? Who are the people you need to be networking with so that you can position yourself favourably? If you don't manage to find a life partner now, will you still have the time and opportunities to do so once the rat race begins? Are you considered a failure if you never end up settling down with a partner and starting a family?

Or, perhaps you're a corporate executive or full-time employee in your mid-twenties to thirties working your daily nine-to-five job. When you first started out, you might have felt excited and driven to finally leave your mark on the world and fulfil your ambitions. But a couple of years later, your life has been entirely segmented into three parts: your day job, the couple of hours at night you have to rest before the next day, and the weekend, where you attempt to make up for all the rest, recreational activities, or social needs that you missed out during the week. Your job pays the bills, but it's become a mechanical task for you to get through every day. It might not necessarily challenge you to grow as a person. It might not fulfil you, or it might not even be something in your interest in the first place—but you had no choice to take it on anyway because the job market was bad, there was pressure on you to be doing something great with your life as a culmination of everything you've learnt after you graduated, and you spent nearly twenty years of your life studying and working relentlessly for a paper degree that only serves to tell your potential employers that you're knowledgeable and a specialist in that particular field of study. Surely you've got to work a job that justifies the amount of money, time, blood, sweat, and tears spent on your formal education at the expense of other pursuits that might be less lucrative, but more fulfilling! Otherwise, what did you give up your dreams for? And the unfortunate thing is, perhaps by the fifth year of your career, you're wondering if it is time to switch jobs or try your hands at something new. And for a while, it does bring a breath of fresh air into your life, but after a period of time, you find yourself back at the same spot again—stuck in an endless loop.

Perhaps you're a fifty-something veteran in your field, and you're looking for change, because you've gotten what you wanted out of your career and realized that there's something more you want out of your life. Perhaps you've realized that you neglected every other aspect of your life apart from your career, and you want to rectify that. Perhaps you're a seventy-something retiree, and you're wondering what else there is to life besides living it day by day as you wait for the day you die.

When you encounter such instances when you question where your life is at, where it is going, what really matters to you, and what your purpose in life really is about at the end of the day, I would like to assure you that it's a step you have taken towards looking inwards at yourself. And as much pain and struggle or joy and happiness as it may bring—**keep going.**

Sometimes, we give up our dreams and settle for less while telling ourselves that what we have is good enough. Sometimes, unfortunate circumstances happen to us and make us give up parts of ourselves. Sometimes, the life that we live does not belong to us, but to the expectations of us, to the intentions of others, and to the popular dreams that are trendy at the moment. We gather these second-hand dreams and ideas that belong to others and try to cobble together what our lives could be and what we desire.

However, the answers don't lie there, but within us. But however well and good our intentions are, in chasing after the lives of others, we reject and deny what is fundamentally at the root of ourselves: *ourselves.*

The term 'mental health' has rapidly gained traction over the last couple of years, especially in the wake of the pandemic, but there is still a large lack of understanding that mental health is a spectrum on which everyone has their own place depending on where they are in their journey. Some of us are battling mental health conditions and illnesses. Some of us are in the middle, where what we're going through is not necessarily deemed severe enough to be classified as an illness or disorder, but we feel the brunt of our symptoms nonetheless in our everyday lives, and it hinders us from thriving and performing at our optimum capabilities when we need to. Some of us are doing relatively well holistically in the different aspects of our lives, and we're looking at how to take it to the next level. Yet, as I say this, I want to emphasise that somebody who is thriving in their lives can absolutely still go through mental health struggles that are specific to their life's circumstances. Likewise, people who struggle chronically with mental illnesses or disorders can absolutely have days where they're feeling good. Essentially, everybody has mental health, and we relate to it in ways that are entirely unique to our circumstances, our psyche, and our history.

Where you fall on the spectrum is entirely unique to you, and that is why resolving your issues is not matter of looking outwards at what people have done to resolve their issues and replicating that—although that can certainly give you more data and clarity on what works and what doesn't—but more importantly about looking inwards, understanding the true nature of the issue (since our external reality is really nothing more but a reflection of who we are inside), and examining the core of who *you* are, so that you can do what *you* need to do to triumph over *your* challenges and live *your* **best** life.

Presently, the world is going through a mental health epidemic. More than ever, people are experiencing increasingly severe bouts of depression, anxiety, and on the most severe end of the spectrum, suicidal thoughts, suicide attempts, and suicide cases. In fact, I want to highlight this particular incident that stands out to me. In 2021, a sixteen-year-old student from River Valley High School in Singapore was charged with the murder of a thirteen-year-old schoolmate. Our world sank when the news was publicly released. He was found to have been previously assessed at the Institute of Mental Health in 2019 after attempting suicide. I believe that this incident highlights the state that children and younger folk are in these days in terms of their mental health and overall wellbeing. There is much more to be done and ground to be covered as this incident happened despite the fact that governmental bodies have been ramping up on incorporating mental health more holistically into schools and workplaces.

It is precisely because of this that we need to tackle the whole issue of mental health not by adopting a blanket one-size-fits-all solution, but by looking inwards, because suicide never happens in a moment. Suicide never ever happens in a moment. There are a million moments leading up to that point. Each moment we choose not to face and deal with questions that matter or bother us, emotions that are 'unpleasant', or conflicts and baggages in our lives, we risk falling or spiralling further down the spectrum. Our issues never really go away until we deal and resolve them at the root level head on.

Our life begins the moment we're born—especially in the moments we can no longer consciously remember. The very first time you opened your mouth and cried out loud as a baby, what were your parents' reactions? What was *your* response to that?

The very first time you displayed any bout of anger or rebellion, what were the reactions of the people around you? Did they talk down to you and reprimand you? Did your parents tell you that a good son or daughter would never have exhibited such behaviours? Were you present to the anger and the subtle shame and guilt that ran inside your programming? What did you learn about your emotions, social behaviours, and boundaries consequently from those incidents? The very first time you cried and wished you had your parents' approval and attention but was left waiting and wanting, what was *your* response to that? What did *you* tell yourself about love and relationships?

The very first time you opened up to a teacher or a family member about your dreams to be an artist, a singer, an astronaut, a designer—what was their response? What was *your* response as a reaction to that? What did *you* tell yourself about dreams and reality? What were *your* notions and beliefs around success?

Perhaps this is about your identity. The very first time you realized that you fell somewhere on the LGBTq spectrum, and you didn't exactly turn out exactly the way your parents or society expected you to be—'normal'—and you chose courage, came out to these people, but were rejected, or the first time you witnessed someone else in a similar boat get rejected and judged by others— what did it teach *you* about family? What did *you* tell yourself about *your* identity? What did *you* tell yourself about courage, and how did it shape your relationship to it?

One of the most common myths we have around pain is that time heals all wounds, but that couldn't be further from the truth. Time makes us forget that those wounds exist in the first place—it gives us the opportunity to evade or numb ourselves with drugs, alcohol, entertainment, or some other form of escapism from our pain, until we forget about them. And sometimes we go into a delusion thinking that these issues are no more. Silly us.

It doesn't matter what the topic is—the very first statements we tell ourselves about that topic grow with us as we grow as people throughout the various stages of our lives, and they get reinforced over time as we encounter similar incidents repeatedly. And oftentimes, while these statements may have served and saved us from pain once upon a time in the very first moment, they tend to do us more harm than good in the long run. For instance, if you've always been told that crying is bad and you were punished for it, you might have resorted to numbing away any nuance of sadness or grief the moment you feel it. Doing that might have saved you punishment from your parents while growing up, but as an adult, that numbing has its repercussions. You might become so numb and disconnected from yourself that you can't tell what matters to you anymore, and you're always looking outwards for answers. Or each time you suppress an emotion just adds another drop into the pressure cooker of emotions inside you that's bubbling and waiting to explode when you least expect it, and when you're least prepared to deal with it.

Emotions have always been a tricky topic that we've not yet managed to successfully incorporate well into our upbringing at home and in the education system. Our understanding of emotions is largely limited to happiness, anger, and sadness, but what about everything else in between? What about the subtle emotions like guilt, jealousy, shame, disgust, contempt, or envy? Not to point fingers at anyone in particular, as most parents and educators are only teaching what they've been taught and what they know, and we simply do not know any better, but some of the most unhelpful advice given to kids in school regarding emotions is to just 'not be sad because it doesn't help' and 'be positive and things will work out'. What we've gotten out of that advice are generations of people who are completely out of touch with their emotions, particularly those that are deemed as 'difficult and unpleasant', and are going through the motions of their lives without ever fully participating, engaging, and involving *themselves* in how it unfolds. This only serves to worsen the mental health struggles we face and potentially turn them into long-term mental health disorders.

The unconventional wisdom is to be able to receive the pain such that the pain completes its course and when the pain no longer has a reason to make you suffer, then perhaps it's time for you to heal. And if you are not busy dying, maybe you will expend some energy into what it takes to live. And if you live, the next question is, how alive do you want to be?

It is crucial to understand that having the ability to manage our emotions is tantamount to managing ourselves as people who are functional and able to contribute value meaningfully to society. It is integral to be able to deal with crisis situations, to being able to lead and work with a team of people from all walks of life with various personalities. It is necessary to be able to connect with another person on a deeper level and hear the things that are left unsaid. It is absolutely paramount to maintaining a healthy overall wellbeing, because a heavy suppression of our emotions eventually leads to damage on our physical body that manifests as various forms of diseases and illnesses.

The repercussions and consequences of not being able to deal with crisis, of not being able to deal with people both in our personal and professional lives, of having our emotional baggage manifest itself as physical diseases such as cancers, diabetes, or even autoimmune diseases can leave a deep negative impact that takes us years to recover from. Some people never really quite recover. Some resign to the fact that their life is filled with woes so much so that they have accepted that this is where and how their lives end, and these are the people who unfortunately never come to the awareness that there is a way out.

I want to say this—**there is always a way out, no matter how bad circumstances present themselves to you.**

Fortunately, if you're finding *yourself* and looking for *your* place in this world, there is a way—your mental and emotional health is a starting point from which you can begin looking into your psyche, your past, your present, how your future will play out, and what you can do NOW to shape them—just as you shape your life, your paths, and your destinies.

Threading Worlds: Conversations on Mental Health is a literary compilation of conversations my team and I have had with seventy-five other contributors in Singapore from March 2021 to May 2021 around the topic of mental health and emotional wellness. These seventy-five contributors come from all walks of life—doctors, nurses, caregivers, counsellors, psychiatrists, therapists, policymakers, social workers, politicians, business leaders, coaches, and youths—and we had facilitated conversations with them on their perspectives on the mental health scene, their own personal journeys, as well as what needs to be done at an individual, community, and national level so that we can move forward and evolve as a collective. Each conversation was transcribed word-for-word with minimised filters deliberately to retain the essence of each conversation such that readers are able to immerse themselves in the conversation and experience it as though they were present in the very moment when the conversation first took place.

This book is intended to serve as a mental and emotional health literacy resource worldwide, and especially in countries like Japan, Korea, and Thailand, where suicide rates are the highest, and third-world countries where looking inwards and the whole idea of mental health is a luxury in relation to the survivalist fights they have to battle each day instead. Through the perspectives from different walks of life, stories of vulnerability, and journeys of recovering and rediscovering oneself, instead of telling people what mental health is and what it is not, we aim to create an immersive experience that allows you to connect to yourself and derive the personal wisdoms and lessons embedded within these stories with your inner-knowing that you can apply to your life. It is best experienced in a distraction-free state when you are able to be *fully and wholly present to yourself* as you experience the book.

As much as you are able to at this moment in your life, I would like to invite you to begin approaching this not exclusively as a mental-health-specific topic, but as a journey of illumination that you embark on to seek the important answers to the questions you have about yourself, your life, and the world around you, so that you can find your footing and live a life that truly matters to you at the end of the day. Many of us, at some point in our lives, ask the bigger questions with heavier weights: Who am I? Where did I come from? What am I meant to do? What is my purpose? What is my truest self? What is the meaning of life itself? And my life? How do I live a worthwhile life?

That is right. This has always been about your life, not just your mental health. When we run so hard trying to find our way out of the overwhelming barrage of circumstances our lives are presented with, we might find ourselves reaching our breaking point and collapsing physically, mentally, emotionally, even spiritually. At times when we are defeated, there is no way upwards but to muster every drop of willpower in us to crawl our way to the door and roll ourselves out.

We live in a world where our actions create a ripple effect down the road. Consequently, there are the forces of cause and effect in play. What matters is not what happens in the past or the future, but what you choose to do right now that consequently affects the trajectory of your life. Every passing moment is a second chance to turn it all around. As the saying goes: 'It is easier to build strong children than to repair broken men.' For us to nurture a generation free from the weight of the pain that we and our ancestors bear, we must first heal ourselves to break out of the chains that bind us. To find ourselves, we must first have the courage to give up what we believe is the truth about ourselves and walk the path of self-discovery. Only then do we know what it takes to make a difference to ourselves, and can we have the power to teach others what it means to be a human being in their own right, and be that beacon of light to those finding their way out of the dark.

Ultimately, my goal is to see a society where people thrive, not just survive, and are empowered to be bold, be free, and be ourselves. To have a conscious connection, not just with another person, but with ourselves. To embark on a journey to seek the answers we're searching for. To dare to dream, and dare to make those dreams happen. To gather our courage and take leaps of faith, even if we don't know where and how we'll land. To confront our deepest fears. To stand on the roof and declare our deepest truths to the world. To strike a pose and shout out to the universe, 'This is Me!' To challenge our adversities. To fail in our quest to live a good and fulfilling life, because it is through those failures that we learn what it means to stand for something that matters to us, time and time again, against all odds. To feel deeply, love deeply, and know that there is absolutely no shame in expressing ourselves authentically—no matter what people think.

One life saved can save many other lives. When we embark on the journey of living a life that truly matters to us, we also empower ourselves to step onto a path that enables us to touch another person's life with our highest being. A path along which we create a future that we're excited to step into, a path where we *live our mark* on the world—so that when the time comes for us to go, we will go not with regrets, but with the knowledge that we have given every drop of our tears, sweat, and blood to living a life true to ourselves.

All of us are a walking morass of questions, on the journey of seeking the answers to living fully alive, and enjoying the ride along the way. Again, to reiterate what I said in the beginning—if by the stroke of luck, a gesture of goodwill, or what have you, something about this book resonated with you, found its way to you, and landed in your hands—let it be a sign that there are certain answers in your life that you're searching for, and may this book be contain some of the lessons and wisdom that can empower you on this journey. When you are done, pass it to another person to pay it forward. Because you never know who may need just that ounce of light to get themselves back on track, since we have adapted to become experts in masking our emotions (I say this sarcastically . . . but this is a very real issue today).

I share this message from a space of love and courage, as somebody who has taken a stand for the transformation of ourselves, transcendence of our limitations, and actualisation of our innate potential. And when the time comes, I look forward to meeting you, the reader of this book, someday—the parts of you that can be a beacon of light to the higher consciousness of this world. May our stories, journeys, and collective wisdoms and transformations inspire even more people to begin looking into themselves so that they can begin their own journey of transformation, so that they live their marks on this world, so that when the time comes for us to go, we will go not with regrets, but with the spirit of the life that we've lived, well with dignity.

Hun Ming Kwang
Founder, Creative Director, Author of ThisConnect.today

'There is No Deadline for Grief'

By Hun Ming Kwang

Among the spectrum of emotions available to us, grief lies at the deeper end. It is an overwhelming intense form of sadness, coupled with a myriad of deep emotions that fundamentally stems from loss.

One of the biggest misconceptions we have in approaching grief, and pain, is that *time heals all wounds*. This misconception happens not only to individuals, but can be seen across our society where things are constantly moving forward at a relentless pace, regardless of ones' state of being. For example, when we suffer a deep loss, such as the death of our loved ones, we usually take a period of compassionate leave from work to plan for the wake and funeral, handle the legal administrative paperwork, and once the funeral is over, we get back to the office, and life goes on. The underlying assumption in this is that we can put a timeline to grief. We are under the impression of a cultural belief that by the end of a three to five days of wake and funeral, that it is time for us to get back to our grind, and time to put ourselves back into our jobs, because *that is what everybody do and it is normal to be doing so*, even if we feel emotionally incomplete. In another vein, this lies

1

another misconception about grief—that it only happens when we experience death.

What many people don't realize is that grief comes in many forms, in particularly during times of change. We can grieve the loss of a loved one—during a romantic breakup, the end of a friendship, the divorce of our parents, and even so when one of our family members move out and away of home. We can grieve the loss of a beloved job, the destruction of nature, the change in our environment where we used to feel a sense of belonging, safety and security. We can grieve the loss of independence, the loss of an opportunity, or the loss of hope for the future. We can grieve for the memories of our childhood we longed for the moment we graduate from school, and when we realize the working world was not all it is made up to be. We can grieve for the dreams we have long given up on, feeling empty and at a loss in the knowledge why and how that we've settled for less in life. We can also grieve during the happiest moments of our lives, wishing the moment would never end just so that we don't have to deal with a different side of reality.

There is a popular framework that tells us how to understand grief intellectually. This framework states that there are seven emotional stages to grief. It usually starts with shock or disbelief, followed by denial, anger, bargaining or justifying, guilt or depression, then acceptance or hope. Just from this framework alone, we can gather that grief comes with a myriad mixed bags of emotions. Commonly known, one tends to withdraw ourselves or to express our sorrows in tears during the phase of grief. The symptoms of grief are not isolated to emotional ones alone. Grief can have a physical effect on our body and health, and in our physical space and environment as well, changing the state of social settings. This is, at the very least, a basic understanding of what grief is, that I've come to known, working personally with all walks of lives by far in the last decade. However, I found it to be true, even for myself, that what most people struggle most with is in unpacking the difficult complex emotions that come with grief. And understandably so, most of us grew up in an environment where emotional literacy was never emphasized, or taught to us.

The layman's definition of emotions may revolve around happy, sad, and angry, which are by nature more recognizable for the erratic, loud expression, and change of tone or states that one can easily pick up. Grief, however, is an extreme form of sadness, more subtle, described as *a black hole in the heart*, and many of us just simply do not know how to deal with an emotion that affects a person at such depth. There are times where the hole feels like there is no end to it. Oftentimes, we only realize the extent to which we have been affected by grief only until a much later stage, usually only when our physical or mental health deteriorates to a severe state. This is why it is important to raise awareness on what grief truly is.

We must first establish that everyone experiences grief in deeply personal and different ways. No two persons can grieve the same way. Some people grieve by mourning openly, others grieve by mourning privately. Some people grieve by talking about the people that have passed or the loss that they've just experienced, while others prefer not to talk about it at all and to deal with it themselves. Some people seek comfort in religion and their social circles, while others question their faith or spirituality. In any case, I personally feel it is about respecting the individual's choice. This chapter does not serve to tell people what is right or wrong. It only serves to give people the awareness and the clarity to put to words the states that they are dealing with, so that they can begin to make a more conscious choice than ever to decide how they would like to move forward, in their lives.

The process of grieving can look like a frightening picture, one that involves leaving something that was so integral to our lives behind. And it is true for the amount of energies, resources, time we have invested in something that we have a deep strong relationship, or simply attachments onto.

Many a times, we console our friends who are grieving with statements like, 'You know what, you'll feel better soon,' or, 'You'll move on eventually'. But the issue with these statements don't necessarily empower or bring comfort to a person, much less to help an individual to go through the process of grief. Our grief does not lessen with time. It is not just about moving on or 'forgetting' that makes us feel better, and it is certainly not about finding closure inappropriately. Afterall, we never really forget the things that ever happened to us since the day we were born. Our muscles have memories, and so does our heart.

So, how can we grieve more effectively? Firstly, we all need a safe space and time to be alone or to get the right help with and for ourselves to process these difficult emotions. This requires us to be present to the grief, to be present to the loss, and to be present to the sudden new reality that we need to adapt to and live by. Part of grieving comes with acceptance, forgiveness, and learning—accepting what is present at this very moment, the changes between the new life and the old, finding forgiveness, especially with ourselves, and learning the lessons that came with the experience so that we can truly gain closure and find completion, rather than brushing and rushing off, thinking that we have moved on. It is certainly difficult, confronting, and that's why we learnt to deny these complex feelings. Just because we don't think about it do not mean we don't feel them. Importantly, we have to remember that grief has no timeline, and time does not heal all wounds.

People who are grieving often end up in a cycle of self-blame, where they wished that the loss didn't happen. This is the stage of bargaining. When we start bargaining and justifying our part to play in the loss, self-blame kicks in. One of the lessons of grief is to accept and to forgive. Accept that things have already happened, and that even if you could change the outcome if you did what you wanted to, the fact of the matter is that you didn't, and the moment had already passed. We can't turn back time. Forgiving yourself comes with making peace with what has happened, and to realize your place and the choices you have made or not made, and the consequences that came with it. Forgiveness also means acknowledging yourself for what you had done in your power when you have had, that you did your best to your ability as much as you could in that given moment. Every moment in our life there lies and presents the lessons that one can learn and take away with. We can never move forward with the newfound lessons in this chapter of life if we do not forgive. We may be tempted to stay and hold on to the past—but do also consider that moving forward also open new possibilities for you to discover and a new journey for you to walk on.

The process of dealing with grieve is never just about moving on. And it is definitely not about returning things to *normalcy*, where everything looks and feels the same *except* for the loss and emptiness. The insistence of being in denial—trying to return things to what they were will only make you more present to the black hole of loss and emptiness within, because the loss becomes that much more real and shakening in this fragmented reality. The process of dealing with grief is about moving forward. We move forward only by accepting things for what they are, so that we can get to where we need to go. We move forward when we don't treat our grief as our enemy. We move forward when we don't impose timelines onto ourselves. We find it easier to move forward if only we allow ourselves to feel, than to brush and deny our feelings aside. We move forward when we don't try to forget, or to reject, or to suppress these difficult emotions and memories. We move forward when we allow ourselves to grieve freely, as we integrate the lessons that was presented from the whole experience.

When we are able to look back upon what we have lost with gratitude—for the memories, for the moments we have shared, for the experience and the wisdom we have gained—we are then capable of bringing the gifts we have received from grief into the next chapter of our lives, and welcome new possibilities and new beginnings.

So don't be afraid of grief.

Find the space you need.

Get help.

CHAPTER ONE

The Strength to Keep Going

By Vickineswarie Jagadharan, Professional Counsellor, OTHERS Speaker and Advocate of Mental Health

Vicki's journey into the mental health field as a professional counsellor was catalysed both by her own empathy towards the struggles teenagers and parents faced, and more significantly the struggles her son experienced, and continued to experience, despite their best efforts to support him out of it before he eventually took his life. As both a mother and a mental health practitioner, Vicki shares about how she moved through her grieving process, and the key aspects of parenting that all parents should never dismiss, when it comes to a child's mental health.

WHAT ARE THE SIGNS?

MK

I heard about your journey. I may not necessarily be able to relate to it because I stand in the role of an observer and third party, but I know how painful that can be. I feel you. That's why I wanted to speak to you to see how your sharing of your personal journey can become a source of light for the bereaved, for those who experienced loss, and for those who are suffering.

Vicki

Thank you for giving me this opportunity. My name is Vicki. I am a school counsellor. Prior to that I was in the corporate line and the calling came up for me to be a counsellor, so I started my journey and finished my education. There were two reasons why I wanted to be a counsellor. Being a teenager, I know the challenges teens would go through, and I saw many teenagers out there, the challenges that they face, the challenges their parents face, and sometimes how working professionals are clueless on how to manage their teams. I realized that it was something I could do. So I decided to take up this counselling course to become a professional counsellor.

But what really pushed me to go further was my son and what he went through regarding his mental health. During our childhood days, we didn't talk much about mental health. It was a period of being happy, laughing, joking around, and we may have had all these difficulties and challenges in the mind—not really knowing how it works—but we never paid much attention because we felt that *eh, just move on.*

But as time went by and evolved, mental health became a very prevalent and apparent issue. People started realizing that there's something off about themselves. They think to themselves *there's something wrong with the way I think, the way I believe, the way I see, the way I feel.* And of course being in this line, I had the knowledge of whatever my son was going through. When he was young, he was a very bubbly boy. His growing years were wonderful and I've come to understand that you don't need to have an intact family for children to grow up from fine young boys and girls into fine young men and women. It all depends on how we nurture them, and show them love, care, and understanding.

As he was growing up, there were external factors that played a part like my ex-husband, and other people who came into his life that could have contributed to what he was going through. You know when teens hit adolescence, they go through a lot of change, hormonal changes, and hit the period of growing struggles and challenges. I believe that he felt stuck in that phase because of what he had been receiving, especially since he was never really one to share much about himself, and in fact kept everything to himself. In certain cultures, it's a common expectation that boys are supposed to be strong, that men don't cry, and any vulnerable expression of themselves is a weakness. Now, I've come to understand that it's something we need to do away with. It is okay for boys to express. It is okay for them to cry and feel, like how girls and women feel.

And I think this part, he probably kept it to himself and didn't want to say much, but I came to find out that he was being bullied in school, and I was very concerned about why he didn't tell me about that, and it accumulated. Sometimes, growing boys are chubby at a certain age, they have baby fat, and sometimes they like to eat a lot as well, so my son was on the plumper side with bits of fat here and there, and I think that caused him to be ridiculed and mocked by his friends. He was pretty upset. When he was thirteen or fourteen and hit secondary school, all of a sudden, he started not wanting to go to school. As I had already started doing my studies in counselling psychology, I was particularly concerned about why he had started not wanting to go to school and asking me to write him a parent's letter. At that time, I didn't really take heed and realize that he was pretty upset about what was happening between my ex-husband and myself.

And it dawned on me that parents can also contribute to a child's mental health if they are not aware of what they say and what they do, because we are living, walking role models.

As I recollected that prior to that he was much more jovial and happy, I knew that there were some changes and I noticed that he just wanted to stay home and he started gaming. As a mother, I was clueless and wanted him to come out of it. I asked him, 'Why are you like this? Snap out of it'.

I knew that he did not want to go to school. He finished his O Levels and did pretty well, but thereafter said 'I don't want to go for this, I don't want to go for that'. So he was pretty upset about whatever was happening with him. I started talking and asking him, 'So what went wrong? Why don't you want to go to school and further your studies?' But he started gaming every night, and only sleeping during the day.

Because I was in this field, mental health, I understood that kids and teenagers go through this phase, possibly because of some triggers, events, and experiences they could have had as they were growing up that affected their mental and emotional wellbeing. And they usually don't express it but bottle it up, which is how they start having their own negative thoughts, assumptions, and forming their own belief systems.

I started talking to him not like a mother, but like a professional with a mother's love. And I told him you know, I think we need to sit down and ask you why this is happening. And because I'm in this line, I knew that people often avoided seeking help because of stigma in our culture and society. I made sure that he got the relevant help from the Child Guidance Clinic in IMH[2]. He went for sessions with tender care and love and family support, and he sort of came out of it while on medication. After that, they weaned him off medication and he was able to function well again. He started going to school. But I think it was comorbid, because he had OCD as

---

[2] IMH: Institute of Mental Health (Singapore's only hospital dedicated to mental health)

well. He was very particular about certain things. Things had to be *very* clean. He was afraid of people seeing and judging him, and these thoughts started coming to him frequently. I tried to speak to him and explain to him that it is all about the way he sees things. What makes him think that people are judging him? Then after some time he sort of understood that, and I helped him to manage his emotions, his thoughts, then he started going to school again. But he still didn't want to mix in with the crowd too much, and he didn't want to take the public transport. So it was a really long journey for him at that period of time, taking it step by step to make sure that he was able to face his fears. He didn't want to touch the doorknobs and all that, so these were the stages I had to slowly take him through, and expose him to things he was fearful of.

After some time, he started going to school and meeting his friends. Then he told me 'Let's move into our own house, let's have more privacy'. Prior to that, I was staying with my parents. So I agreed, 'Okay, if you want to we will get our own home'. And I noticed that there were still changes—he took a very long time when he went to shower and sort of didn't talk much to everyone and mostly kept to himself in the room. At certain times, keeping up his personal hygiene was an issue for him as well. I told him you still gotta do the necessary basic things like having your shower, coming out, cleaning your room. So with tender loving care, step by step, I took him through. As a caregiver, it was not very easy for me because I myself was a bit drained. You can't give from an empty cup, right? I was really drained at that period of time. But because I love my son, and I wanted to do my best for him, I know that it was . . . You see, the thing is that, whatever he was going through, he didn't ask for it. It's just that it happened, same for a lot of people who were going through it.

Eventually, we moved into our new house and he was very happy. He also took up a part-time job, he completed his diploma in Mass Communications and was into taking his degree thereafter. So he was fine, going for part-time work and all that. But after some time, I noticed that there was a change in him once again. So I wondered what this change was about and he said 'My friends are calling me, wanting to go out.' So I said, 'Why don't you go?' He said 'No lah, I don't feel like going because each time I go I gotta ask you for money and I know you're financially a bit cash-strapped, it's so difficult for you.'

I think he understood that I was also struggling a bit because as a single mum, I had to pay for the house, the bills, and all that. Then he became very conscious about his body image and he was very restrictive of his food intake. I used to tell him 'Don't starve yourself, maybe you should eat healthly.' So I helped him to prepare his food. One thing is that he was very diligent, so he prepared his food and all that. Wonderful boy, wonderful son, he helped me with the chores around the house, he did a lot of cleaning. He was very particular about cleanliness. Extremely. Sometimes, he didn't open up the windows and when I asked why, he said 'No, people will see.' That's how I knew that he was struggling again.

He did excessive exercise and he liked to eat, but the more he ate, the more he felt that 'I'm eating too much, binge eating'. He went into that kind of cycle. I spoke to him and asked him what exactly he wanted. He said he wanted to come out of it but he didn't know how. He felt stuck somewhere. There were times I saw him struggling. He was so quiet and there were times when we got into arguments because he was stuck somewhere, didn't know how to come out of it, clueless, going in cycles. He was so helpless in those moments. As a mum when I saw him, I felt very very upset and I cried and broke down in front of him sometimes, and I know that he felt so much inside of him as well, but he just didn't know how to express himself, and didn't know what to do.

Faith is very strong value for both of us, so we prayed and we just left it that God will guide and shed some light. As time went by, he didn't want to continue his education. So at that period of time, I wanted him to do what he was interested in. I never really thought that there were other ways to go about it. Now, I tell students and parents that it is okay if the child is not ready to study now. Give them the time because education has no limit. They can also do hands-on things. Some people are not so inclined to academics. Some people like more hands-on activities, maybe business-related things like hairdressing or baking, or just simply doing something that they enjoy. Let it be anything. Then I asked myself if my son would have had that interest as well. Maybe I didn't explore much, or maybe I didn't give him the time to think of all this. So now when I look back and I tell myself, I say yeah, now I know where the gaps I could have at least done better are, but what I knew at that time, I did my best then.

MK

What happened to him?

Vicki

It was a very crucial time when he started becoming very quiet in the last few weeks of that particular period before he took his own life. He didn't want to talk much. I didn't feel that anything was amiss when this took place that particular day. We had a very close bond. I would tell him that I love him, he would tell him that he loved me. We hugged and talked a lot. He would ask me about my own work. He said, 'Ma, I want you to go out and help others because I know that's your passion. I want to come out of this but I do not know how to. How come, mama, you are so positive, even when I tell you certain things?'

So, I said that we need to see positives in everything. Even in negatives, there is something there. Even hardships, good times, bad times, nothing is permanent—it just comes right after another. We just need to sit and see what we can do about it instead of worrying about it and cracking our heads. So think about what we can do, and what we can do, we will try our best. And if we can't, then it's okay because things change. Nothing is permanent, things change. And today, *it's okay not to be okay*. I told him that. And what happened was the usual; we texted each other.

So that particular day in 2015, second of March, I went to work as usual and he was playing his game in the morning and he told me, 'Ma, come back quickly, I love you'. And I told him I loved him as well. Then I went off to work. Normally before I came back, I would call him to find out how he's doing, or he would call me to ask what time I would be back. So I called him and he didn't answer the phone and that sort of made me feel uneasy. Normally he would. Then I came back home as per normal at five o'clock and I rang the doorbell, and there was still no answer. I was wondering, what happened? He's not even answering. So I had the key and I opened the door.

The moment I opened the door, I saw my son on the platform on his knees. He was pretty tall. I just ran to him and I just—my whole world shattered. I screamed. I cried. I don't know what exactly happened, what I did—I just saw my son there. I had a rattan swing. He used the belt to hang himself there. I just. I was clueless. Shattered. Running from where he was to my prayer room and the only thing I said was 'God, please forgive my son'. I really didn't know what to do. There was even a feeling at that moment, *should I end my life as well?* But I knew that I wasn't supposed to be doing that. My faith didn't tell me to do that. What I did was to take the scissors to cut the belt and bring him down. I put him on the floor and I was just looking at him, not knowing what to do next because the belt was in his neck and I didn't want to hurt him anymore. I informed my parents and I just sat there for fifteen to twenty minutes. I was just there.

My neighbours came by and they were pretty shocked. Then the paramedics came and I didn't know what I was doing. I was just moving around . . . and of course we had the Catholic ceremony, the rituals, the wake, and all that. It was only after a few days when it really dawned on me that yes, my son is not with me anymore. Yup, my son is not with me now. It hit me hard.

The reality that he's no longer there physically . . . It took me a while. I was away from work for a month and a lot of days I cried, asking myself why, what was happening, was there something I could have done or was there something . . . how come I didn't know? There was no clues, no signs. I started blaming myself. Thereafter, there were many nights that were so difficult to understand, about why this whole thing had to happen. I was in denial. Why couldn't he have come out of it? He wrote a note telling me that 'Ma, I want you to carry on with life. I want you to move on, I want you to go and help others.' I understood his pain yet I couldn't. It was hard to swallow that truth. It was too much for him to bear.

Over time, I realized the pain never got away. I missed him. I eventually told myself that yes, time may not heal my pain. As time goes by, the pain gets lesser and lesser, but it will always be there. Because he is my son, my child. We're moulded by the pain. You know we normally go through the grief process, right? The bargaining, the acceptance, and then the denial, and all that. Being in this mental health and counselling profession, I know that these are the stages. It took many years till today, and eventually I managed to get back on my feet, yes. I think it was my faith that kept me together and brought me back and at the same time. This chapter gave me the drive, the passion inside myself to do more—that it's one life too many and I wanted to do something for the many humans out there. I told myself that yes, I'm going to do what my son told me in his final words to me, that 'I want you to go and help others.'

I started this journey to advocate for mental health with a stronger conviction that I wanted to do something. Of course, now I'm in a secondary school, and I'm doing what I love doing—looking out for the kids and the children there, and their parents as well. It's a long journey. And I know that a lot of awareness needs to be raised and people need to normalize it just like physical pain. When we have physical pain, we go and see a doctor. We don't hesitate. So why is it that when we have pain in the heart, in the mind, when we're emotional, we don't go and seek help? I think there should be more awareness to move away from this stigmatization, become less judgemental, and know that it's okay that sometimes we go through hard times where we have these mental health struggles. So what does it mean for mental wellness? It's more of not judging, being who you are, loving yourself, caring for yourself, and of course it starts from the family, from parents, from children, the community, the society at large. And I think if we all come together, we can work something out. And at the same time, if everyone puts their mind to it, I think we can help a lot—a lot of children, and even parents as well—to do away with the stigma. So that many will come and seek help, just like for any other ailments. When you're physically disabled or anything like that, you can see it and you show empathy and kindness. But what happens if you're emotionally affected? You can't see it because your perspective could be limited. Everyone may appear to look normal outside but when you talk to them, but when you attempt to listen, to understand, to see deeply, you see their behaviours, then you come to understand that they may be going through some challenges, and they may be going through struggles, and they need attention and help. Sometimes they're so afraid to ask for help because they're afraid of being judged. They're afraid of how society will look at them. They're afraid that they may not get jobs. They're afraid of how people will see them. That's why they keep to themselves. They're silent about it and they don't want to tell anyone. Until someday later, when another life will be gone.

So, I've started on this journey. I want to persevere in this journey, and I want to tell myself that it is for me as well. There was a time when I felt very upset and down, and I would ask myself 'Why am I feeling all this? Is it because of what I went through? Why me, of all people? Why, my child?'

I had to seek help as well. I am only human, and there are times where we human beings fall and falter, and we do need to get our treatments. Even our doctors and nurses fall sick too on their bad days. So what about counsellors? The professionals in the helping profession are also human beings. They also need help. I went and sought help to understand myself better. To process my grief. Then I could move on with my journey. Accepting that this has happened, so what can I do next to help myself and help others? There could be many out there who are suicide survivors as well.

Vicki

MK, thank you so much for giving me this opportunity to share. I am really grateful to be able to be in this space with you. Looking back at it, yes it was very painful because he was my one and only son. But I know that the dream he and I had shared for me to go on and help others is something that I hold very dearly to me. I know self-care is also very important, and I would like to emphasize that to many out there. Look out for the signs and symptoms. Never dismiss anything when a child says something. Because back in my days when parents hear it, they will say 'Aiyah go and die lah'. Sometimes, we are quick to dismiss and we may not step into the shoes of those who are suffering and bearing those pain. Many years back, it was not taken very seriously but these days, because they're exposed to so many things. For example, social media is one big area and they find it so difficult to grapple with a different reality and circumstances. They are in this technology era that we parents may not be born in, so it's different. My heart goes out to them. My heart really goes out to them. That's why I want to do my little bit, like what Mother Theresa said, do small things with great love. So I'm just trying my best to see how I can help along my journey. That's why I'm currently in a school and doing the best that I can. And of course I'm just asking the almighty God to see what's my next chapter, what I can do next to help. I'm also embarking on another six-month course. Let's see what my journey is after that as well.

MK

Thank you, Vicki. Thank you for your sharing with me your personal journey and pouring your heart out, and trusting me and my work. Let's inspire and reach out to more people with your story.

CHAPTER TWO

To Heal and Love is to Own Our Existence in All its Darkness and Light

By Kyl Lim Yan Keng, Art Psychotherapist, Singapore Cancer Society

As an art therapist in the Singapore Cancer Society, Kyl works with cancer patients who are grappling emotionally with their diagnosis. Many cancer patients deal with feelings of shame and a diminished sense of identity and self-worth because of their illness. The financial burden of seeking treatment may also result in isolation and blame within the family, resulting in feelings of abandonment among cancer patients. Kyl shares that it is a human condition to be flawed, and that behind the scenes, doctors and mental health professionals have their own struggles too.

THE PSYCHOLOGICAL DISLOCATION OF A CANCER DIAGNOSIS

MK

What made you decide to join the Singapore Cancer Society (SCS) as an art psychotherapist?

Kyl

I believe a lot of it has to do with my internship. I served a one-year internship at SCS during my second-year postgraduate art psychotherapy training. It was a wonderful opportunity for me to meet various people from different walks of life, be it my colleagues or my patients who have taught me to be a better therapist and person. I was thoroughly enjoying my work and myself. I felt very comfortable facilitating the sessions. I thought it was a perfect fit as I was able to marry my interests, psychology and art, with helping others. I have always wanted to be very involved in contributing back to society as well as in improving the quality of lives of those individuals I have the opportunity to help. So when there was the opportunity for me to join, I grabbed onto the chance. So here I am, two years later.

MK

What are the mental health challenges and stigmas that you've observed among cancer patients?

Kyl

Before I get into that, maybe I'll touch a little bit on mental illness and social stigma. So mental illness has historically been associated with stigma, and a clinical diagnosis of a mental illness often triggers different responses and attitudes from people of different origins, religions and cultures. They usually hold a considerable impact on people. Besides that, people who carry a particular diagnosis may experience shame, psychological disequilibrium or social stigma, further impacting the way they cope with their symptoms, the level of treatment response, openness, treatment adherence, and also their motivation to seek help, be it from mental health providers, therapists or physicians.

So the particular population I'm currently working with is cancer survivors—although I also work with palliative and hospice cases—and as you know, in Singapore, being an Asian country, we cannot deny that there are very conservative beliefs that surround us. According to research, in most Asian cultures, we practice and we value conformity to norms, emotional self-control, and family recognition through achievement. And because of this, the clinical diagnosis of mental illnesses usually brings with it a host of other crippling issues such as deep feelings of humiliation, loss of face, and a diminished sense of identity or self-worth. It's very prevalent especially in Singapore as a collectivist country, things like social rejection and family shame.

And Asians often believe that all these mental problems are brought about by defective family genes, supernatural influences, magical thinking and also punishments from God, be it bad karma or due to a result of weak character or immoral deeds from previous lives. And receiving a cancer diagnosis can be in and of itself a harrowing and traumatic experience accompanied by turbulent emotions during treatment and beyond. Very often, these cancer patients experience some form of psychological dislocation especially in the acute cancer survivorship. Most of them are able to restore their psychological equilibrium, reconstruct their premorbid psychological health, and recover from their cancer experiences with the appropriate and corrective measures and treatments. With this group of survivors, they grow in the aftermath of the cancer experience with renewed faith, wisdom, and more resilience than before.

There are others, who are less fortunate, who are sometimes unable to recuperate these losses. They suffer more significant physical, psycho-emotional and social impairments and I would say that they also suffer more from social stigma. For example, even if they do want to reach out to counsellors or social workers or even therapists, there are several concerns and self-limiting beliefs that hold them back. One of it is financial concerns. The other one could be gaslighting from their own family members. They would think that . . . How should I put it? They would think that seeking or even taking care of mental health, is for the 'mental,' the 'crazy ones,' the 'nutcases'. And so, these individuals continue to suffer in silence. I have cancer patients who are abandoned by their families due to their conditions, due to financial burdens. Some of them are shunned away from their families. Like what I said earlier on, they are being shamed and gaslit by their loved ones for their emotional mood state, for feeling emotional due to familial conflicts, and the side effects of their cancer treatment (hand neuropathy, leg numbness, 'chemo brain' and etc.). They're shamed for seeking counselling, by so-called family members who are supposedly the people who are the closest and dearest to them, who are supposed to offer a safety net and uncompromising support.

Usually when a member in the household is affected, his or her greatest source of support and resources to carry on is familial support, not the cancer treatments, not the drugs, not the clinician. Imagine having that taken away from them. Can you imagine how vulnerable that leaves them? Who do they turn to in times of grief and sorrow? How do they cope? How do they make sense of the world now that it is them against the world, them against this chronic, life-threatening illness? We are not even talking about the ones who live alone. There are also others who are suffering from loss of identity, dissociation, emotional traumas, marital issues, adjustment challenges, sexual dysfunctions, depression, emotional dysregulation, psychological disequilibrium and suicide ideation. But they are resistant to seeing a therapist, psychiatrist or taking medications due to the fear of carrying a diagnostic label, drug dependency, treatment costs, being judged by others as mental or perceived as though there's something fundamentally wrong with them. For male cancer patients, most of them feel embarrassed and are fearful of being judged for seeking a sexologist, they are also the ones who continue to suffer in silence. They feel ashamed about reaching out and stepping forward. When we don't do the right thing and take care of ourselves, people around us suffer alongside us. It's a ripple effect.

There are also others who dare not declare their cancer diagnosis for fear that they might be treated very differently by their employers and colleagues. I've heard stories where my cancer patients get discriminated against and ostracized at their workplaces. Some of their employers have asked them to quit. Some of them keep their illness a secret as they fear that their employers will reject them based on their condition. Some of them are forced to leave their company when they didn't do anything wrong. It's heartbreaking. Truth is, they fell sick, took leave of absence to take care of their health and when they returned to work, they were being told to leave as though their illnesses were some kind of personal failure. What about their merits? Society can be a very unforgiving place. Cancer patients, just like anyone of us, just want to be and deserve to be treated like a normal human being with equal rights to thrive.

DEALING WITH THE SHAME OF HAVING AN ILLNESS

MK

There are so many recurring issues on the ground that hold patients back from seeking for help and support, and being able to ontologically know what is right and necessary for them because they simply don't feel that they're in a dignified place more than anything else . . .

I'm just wondering, do patients overcome that sense of shame before they ask for help, or do they still experience it as they are going through the treatments?

Kyl

I'm sure there are people who are still stuck in the same spot, probably held back by this great sense of shame and self-limiting beliefs that they experience on the inside. So far, with my experience with my cancer patients, I see that they have stepped out of that sense of shame. It comes with time and I think it's also how their friends and how media can help them better understand that actually, there's no shame in seeking help, be it through counselling or therapy, because it's been a bit more normalized now, I would say. But of course, I still have patients who shy away from this topic. It really boils down to the people they surround themselves with as well, especially when their family members are more of the traditional ones.

MK

Got it.
[MK sighs]

So, I know that for these therapies to be effective, the individual has to be 100 per cent present, 100 per cent willing. And some of these emotional factors that they feel, like shame and rejection, might hold them back from fully participating in the mental health treatment process. How do you think we can reduce that?

Kyl

I think the first step for them is to understand what shame is, the factors causing them to feel shame, and the impact of shame. It's important for them to understand that shame leads people to hide and self-conceal. Actually, people who feel ashamed tend to hide a lot. They dare not develop friendships and never share their true selves with the world. It's also very important to allow them to understand that shame is one of the lowest vibrational frequencies besides fear and guilt and it is a powerful emotion that has the potential to shape people's lives in significant ways. Shame as a secondary self-conscious emotion is experienced by people who cannot move on from their past mistakes, by people who commit reprehensible crimes, live in addiction, or experience stigmatized mental illness. Social stigma and discrimination can worsen mental health problems and prevent a person from getting the help they need. Psychoeducation is an effective way that allows them to understand how shame can be a factor that hinders them from stepping forward.

And I mean, individuals who experience shame to a certain extent, they must also be feeling depressed, anxious, nervous, worthless or helpless. So I think it's also letting them know that these are very normal situations that everyone experiences. I think helping to create these themes of universality and shared humanity and trying to normalize these situations can make them feel safer, less alone, and lead to lesser self-isolation.

THE RIPPLE EFFECT OF STRENGTH BEGINS WITH A DROP OF VULNERABILITY

MK

Got it. And how do you think, as a community, we can do better in this to support people who are going through treatment?

Kyl

What we can do is we need to create—

MK

Safe spaces.

Kyl

Safe spaces. We need to provide these types of holding environments where individuals feel they won't get judged, where they can be themselves and move out from their self-loathing and into the open, where it's okay to let everything out.

I run group therapies, and I've seen people drop out because they are so fearful of being exposed that they cannot take it. For the rest who stay on, there is a ripple effect. Once they see people open up, it just automatically helps them open up as well. I've actually run groups where in the first session, all of them broke down and it was very shocking for me as an intern because I didn't know cancer patients were so denied of that space to be themselves and a lot of times, I hear so many stories where they feel it's important for them to wear a mask or shield their true selves from their loved ones. They don't want to be a burden, they don't want to upset others, and a lot of times they will tell me that actually, being in the group therapy helps them so much more than their own family members because they don't understand and have not experienced what other cancer patients have gone through. Universality is one of the strongest therapeutic values in group therapy.

MK

Can you tell me more about that?

Kyl

It's taking a small risk. So once they are able to test the waters, they self-disclose a bit more and they see that 'Hey, actually, I'm still accepted, there's nothing wrong'. Then it helps them to move out of their fears, all these internalized feelings of shame, humiliation and disgrace and that's one thing that they can do. The other one is developing self-compassion. It's also one way individuals can move out of shame.

And it's also taking the first, small step to healing in the right direction. Surround yourself with the right group of people who are not there to invalidate or gaslight you, make you think twice, or there to shame you.

[silence]

Kyl

I think another way to answer your question is more towards how do we—

MK

As a community—

Kyl

As a community, help to reduce this stigma, isn't it?

MK

Correct.

Kyl

So having said that, we do see that the demand for therapy is growing as it becomes more normalized. The new perspectives that therapy offers can give us valuable self-insight into approaching our lives in a positive and productive way. A lot of times it is not about learning new things. It is about unlearning and relearning. We need to unlearn our conditioned responses, self-limiting beliefs, behaviour and thinking in order to recondition ourselves. There is nothing more noble than becoming superior to your former self. In fact, there are affordable resources that people can go to. We can see that there's an increase in the number of people who are coming forward to create mental health awareness and there's no shame in sharing. And I don't think this is just happening in Singapore, it's happening globally, and I think that youngsters are stepping out more and more to share it publicly, through social media. And for Singapore as a collectivist country, it may take a longer time to embrace this new shift as compared to our individualist contemporaries due to sociocultural differences, but I think that because everyone is sort of embracing this new shift, it also helps one to feel that 'Hey, actually there's nothing wrong with sharing this. This is quite a common issue faced by others too'. This reinforces shared humanity or universality and takes away feelings of isolation. It can inspire others to open up.

BEING WHOLE AND ONE WITH YOURSELF

MK

Got it. Is there a message you would like to say to the public where mental health is concerned?

Kyl

Yes there is. I think it's important that we all understand that in this world, no one is perfect. It's a human condition to be flawed and we are actually all broken in one way or another to a certain degree. Behind the scenes, everyone struggles in some area of their lives, even doctors and mental health providers. It's okay to be broken as long as the brokenness does not interfere or cause hindrances to our personal growth, to our personal relationships and our daily activities.

By sharing this, it's my sincere intent to inject a little bit more honesty and reality into this world of carefully curated social media feeds, where what you see may not actually be what you get. And I think it's important that we start a conversation about our struggles and the overtures required to achieve inner peace and self-transcendence. I also want to share that when we are down with flu, cough, fever, we see a doctor to get better. When we are psychologically overwhelmed, underwhelmed, or ill-equipped to handle life at large, should we not see a mental health provider? Should we not see a therapist? Why shouldn't we treat our mental health the same way? All healing work teaches and guides us to the path of light from a place of darkness. I can't speak for other therapeutic modalities, but one thing for sure I know about art psychotherapy is that it is key to creative living, managing our blind spots, emotional terrains, brokenness, and neurodiversities without being bounded by any prescriptive, intellectual shackles. Confronting our past, and revisiting unhealed wounds prevents us from acting out and also allows the rise of consciousness, and self-awareness from within that forecloses our own destructiveness. Owning one's existence in all its darkness and light enables the potential for past raptures to heal, ancient traumas to loosen its grip, and enables us to love from within, helping us transform into better versions of ourselves to lead a more fulfilling life with all its negative and positive equivalences more bearable. Making the uncontainable, more containable.

So what I want to say is that friends, or anyone out there, don't be afraid of seeking help, don't put off help. Don't be embarrassed about asking for help. And there's absolutely no shame in taking care of your mental health and it's very important that we remember that we all benefit when our own cup is filled first. Start today. Make self-care a priority. Say to yourself, 'I choose to rise above this. I choose to meet life head on. I choose to look after my mental health the way I look after my physical and my spiritual health'. Make your wellbeing and healing a top priority. Have the courage to create boundaries that will support your flourishing. Listen closely to your intuition, respect your need for rest (you don't have to earn it), and connect with people who are emotionally mature. Being intentional with your life is loving yourself well. Embrace your fundamental (not self-limiting) beliefs and values, and then actively redirect and live your life in a way that is aligned with those values. Tapping into your value system on a daily basis sparks the difference between living life passively and living it intentionally.

MK

That was powerful. Because it came from your deepest truth. You can hear the way you're saying it. It was very powerful. And I hope to be able to bring that intention that you shared with me to the world.

Kyl

Yeah, I think you're right. It's because it's from the bottom of my heart.

MK

If the book can stop one person from jumping down, I think we've done our job.

Kyl

Yeah, you're absolutely right!

MK

And that's the intention and space that we come from. Financially, there are better ways to do it and there are options.

Yet this is exactly what is missing in our society today in terms of mental health, emotional wellness, stuff like this. Emotional literacy, how about that? That's missing in our education system.

Kyl

Yes! There's such a huge lack of emotional literacy in our society.

MK

Correct, and oftentimes these emotions that we don't quite understand create a lot of problems in our mental and emotional states. And oftentimes they're psychosomatic and would have manifested physically in a person's body as disease. You've probably heard of it before in your practice. It's all a function of our emotional baggages being a trigger, being a catalyst to something that is happening within the body. We start seeing that our lack of understanding of our emotions creates a spillover into our physical system or even our mental system as well.

Kyl

Yes, yes. They're all linked and what you touched on is really potent and also very important. Psychosomatic ailments, we see a lot of it happening in the world. A lot of ailments don't have a physical cause to it. Medical research has shown that 90 per cent of the illnesses and diseases are stress-related. Doctors can't find the pathological causes, can't diagnose what's wrong after running numerous tests but patients continue to present valid symptoms and somatic complaints. So the next sensible hypothesis would be the possibility of psychosomatic ailments.

MK

And to understand how to address the root cause requires us to understand our emotions. We have to understand what we're really feeling. That means our understanding of emotions cannot be as generic and vague like 'I'm feeling happy', 'I'm feeling sad', 'I'm feeling angry'. We need to talk about the layers within those emotions.

Kyl

Yes, it's very important that one is equipped with a wider emotional vocabulary and I feel that there are so many people who are so emotionally detached and emotionally avoidant. They don't want emotions, they see them as weaknesses.

MK

Or irrelevant, so they cut themselves away from it.

Kyl

Yes, exactly! The moment they cut it off, that is where it becomes a breeding ground for a host of other mental-health-related conditions.

MK

Infestation and things like that start happening. And that's why the things that we haven't really sorted out over the past few years become a can of worms. And of course people are afraid of that! Because it was all this suppression and avoidance that created it. We're cutting a part ourselves away and those things continue to grow!

Kyl

Yes! And a lot of people don't get it. They feel oh if I block my negative emotions—

MK

Then they don't exist.

Kyl

Right! What they don't realize is that at the very same moment they cut themselves off from their emotions, they are actually denying or rejecting parts of themselves too. They're no longer a wholesome person. To heal ourselves, sometimes we have to do the opposite of what we intuitively want to do. We might intuitively want to disconnect from our pains because it is too much for us to bear and it is hard to handle it. We might shut down these negative emotions. But when we do this, we also shut down the positive emotions, the positive side of ourselves. The thing is that we cannot selectively shut down parts of ourselves. That's why it is important to pay attention and expand our awareness to those negative emotions without rejecting them.

MK

If not, you can't be complete.

Kyl

Yes! Exactly. And they engage in a lot of maladaptive coping behaviours.

MK

It's just avoidance. The root issue is still there. The can of worms is still under the carpet.

Just because we put on a beautiful carpet over it, doesn't mean what's underneath is no longer there anymore. In fact, it's still there. Someday it will pop up and say hello! And the problem is, you never know when they will come out and sometimes they don't come out one after another. They come out in packs and gangs, and by then it's too much for a person's psychology to handle. And sometimes to a person contemplating suicide, all they want to do is to escape the pain because in their reality, all they're seeing are four walls of mess and they just want to end that suffering without really consciously realizing that they are ending their lives, because the mess that they're dealing with is much more than what they can handle in life.

We suppress and run away from our stuff. Instead of dealing with our stuff, we run away. We find justifications. We create reasons for ourselves not to look into our own mess and we think that by finding a partner it will cure our problems, for example. Some people believe that.

Kyl

Yeah, they feel that someone needs to complete them.

MK

Correct, without realizing that they need to be complete themselves, and completing themselves requires them to make peace with whatever they cut away.

Kyl

Which also involves ego strength. To do that, we need to have ego strength in order to open up that can of worms. I have patients who are not ready for this. They're not ready for the plumbing work. We also want to be mindful of our readiness to change. Are we really ready or not? Are we really ready to look deeply into ourselves and our emotions even if it is difficult?
[short pause]

Kyl

I don't know if I properly answered the stigma question!
[Kyl laughs]

MK

I think you did. Your perspective was very interesting. I would say it is a very fresh perspective that not a lot of people bother to see unless they're on the ground working with patients.

It's been a privilege this last hour. I enjoyed myself in this conversation. It was thought-provoking.

Kyl

Me too! I found it was as well. Thank you so much for providing this great platform and opportunity for me to share my very humble opinions and story.

CHAPTER THREE

How Do You Show Up For Yourself?

By Sujata Tiwari, Entrepreneur, Life Mentor, Author, Co-Chair of the Mental Wellbeing Interest Group, Singapore International Chamber of Commerce

When her daughter became a victim of rape, Sujata found herself in the challenging position of standing up for her daughter and her family's justice. Though the process was tough, the entire episode now represents for Sujata a symbol of resilience and strength. Her story reminds us of the importance of first standing up and showing up for our mental health.

IT ALL BEGINS FROM CHILDHOOD

MK

The first thing is, Sujata, we want to ask you a couple of questions around mental wellness itself. And having gone through your own journey, what was it like for you to overcome some of these internal battles that you faced?

Sujata

Ah, battles. So the way I look at it or go about it is from childhood. I have learnt that today, when you interact with people who could be belittling you, putting you down, or bullying you—it all starts from childhood. What I want to mention here is that people think children are angelic creatures. They are not. At a very early age, a child learns to survive. If the child is an introvert for example, or is not very sure or confident, the child is going to rely on support by going to her parents or teachers—a grown-up.

Now, what I have seen from childhood is that you may not have this communication with your parents when you feel confident because sometimes what happens with parents—and this happens a lot with boys—is that you're told to follow a certain pattern. Girls can cry, boys are told from an early age 'Don't cry, be a man'. Now, that is something which is very wrong in our society because we are building up a child to not come and share openly, and to live with guilt and shame instead. What if he or she is abused? What if the child has parents who are very strict, who don't understand and keep the communication channel open, and let the child know that they can talk about anything? That no matter what happens, they will not be orphaned? In most cases, children feel that they'll be punished and are hesitant to share as a result of that.

So what happens when you keep it to yourself? That builds up an abusive situation for yourself, if you're not confident that you can tackle it on your own. And that has been my experience. So from childhood, I learnt to just deal with it on my own. I had a single parent since I was brought up by my mother. There was nothing about which I could not say, 'Go and tell her'. I may have chosen not to tell her because she was a widow and struggling on her own, so I tried not to burden her and be self-reliant as much as possible and deal with it. And that's how I learnt to deal with human behaviour and psychology.

So if you were to try to shame me and put me down, or anything, I will rise to it. That's been my experience. When I was young, I was ridiculed for having teeth which were stained, and children are often told 'Oh, you're so fat or you're so skinny' at a tender age. These things that we think are light-hearted statements actually shape the psyche of a child who takes it all up to adulthood and tries to see how they can attain that ideal figure. If they're fat, they try to become thin. If they're thin, they try to put on weight. These are all territories which lead to a certain age where there are things like body shaming. For example, if I take the glamourous world of models and stars, we all look at their hourglass figures, but that all comes with a price. Don't think that it comes just like that—they have to do a whole lot of things to maintain that kind of look. Does it answer your question?

ONLY YOU CAN STAND UP FOR YOURSELF

MK

Would you like to share about your own personal experiences as you were going through life itself? You can share whatever you're comfortable with. I read your book.

Sujata

You read my book? All of it? Then you're a fast reader!

MK

Almost done! But for some of the readers, they may not necessarily understand the case. Would you mind sharing a little bit about the case itself so that they have more context?

Sujata

The case was very simple. My daughter was raped, and when she was raped, the question we faced every time was, do you go, or do you not go and fight it out in the Court of Justice? Because that is the most important thing and she was not in the condition to make a decision. I had to make the decision and I made the decision that we were going to fight it out—and that is what I did. So from talking to the cops, and filing that first information— that was the ultimate step, something which didn't only affect the victim but the whole family as well. And somebody had to step up and decide what to do, for everybody to heal.

Now, at that point in time, it was a split-second decision I had to make. Do I go and fight it out in the Court of Justice? Or do I brush it under the carpet? Brushing it under the carpet would have meant that all of us would have had a lot of emotional baggage. We would never have been able to move on in life and the victim, especially, would always be looking over her shoulder. Who knows about this? What will come out? Who gets to know? She would never find the confidence that she was not guilty or somehow responsible for it because that's what society tells us, right? And I decided that I was not going to do that. So I did not know whether I was going to go to Justice or not because that was a very daunting thing, but I just decided that I would do the right thing—to stand up and say 'Abuse happened and I do not condone it'. And since there was a framework in the law and the judiciary, I went for it.

MK

How old were you at that point in time?

Sujata

It happened seven years back. I was in my fifties, but age is not a criteria for any human emotional trauma or tragedy. Maybe in some cases it is easier to handle but this kind of thing, it doesn't matter whether you're a six-month-old baby—parents still have to deal with it. Or whether you're a seventy-year-old nun. Imagine what they would be going through! So this is one of the most traumatic experiences that one can go through, and it's also a crime so it's easier to deal with because this crime is easily punishable. But what happens when there is bullying or there is psychological and mental abuse for which there is not always a police station you can go to? That, you have to deal with on your own within the framework of the relationship—whether it's inside the house or it's in the workplace. Whether you're in a domestic violence abuse situation, marriage, or something like that. It's very hard because unless you're ready to walk out and are willing to come out, it's tough. Because then what do you do? You have to deal with it on your own, and that is one of the toughest challenges. So in that case if you don't want to call it out, you don't want to shout out, then you have to be prepared for you to handle it on your own until you're ready to walk. So when I made the decision, I just took it and I knew I would go through it. And it was tough. It was very very tough. For seven years, I went through it. Going to work every day was not easy. It just was not easy. It was one of the hardest things you can go through alone. That's what I did.

You have to go through the police, the judiciary, the society who will just put you outside in a box. It's one of the most lonely experiences. But as you can see, from the fact that I'm sitting in front of you and talking to you, that I've overcome it. I'm not going anywhere based on my courage and resilience. That is something we all have. It all depends on how strong we are and how weak we are. Because if you give in to it, then that weakness takes over. You do make a choice, and it's not that you have to punish yourself for being weak, but if you take it forward and rethink and say 'I am going to do something about it', you can always change the course of your actions rather than live with it for years and years. People don't come out of relationships for years, and for years they suffer all kinds of issues like psychological issues, marital issues, or feeling suicidal and depressed. These things just continue all the time, depending on what choice you make.

So that was it. So I had to make the decision. I had to go to the cops and go through the entire thing, which was a very arduous process.

MK

There was a lot of questioning.

Sujata

There's a lot of questioning you have to go through! You have to go through court, you have to go every day, if you want to fight it.

MK

And in India itself, the system is not that effective in solving crimes.

Sujata

Everywhere the system is, the victim indirectly becomes the accused. What happens is the first question is, 'What happened? What were you doing?' Suppose you've gone out late at night or you were drinking. They will ask you those questions that they should not ask. A crime was committed if the victim says 'I have been raped and it was against my wishes'. That should be enough because according to the legal books, that is the premise of the complaint but in reality, it doesn't happen that way. In reality people just go over and over again and the lawyers have the discretion to ask this whether it's in the US, whether it's in India, whether it's anywhere else. I can tell you, having worked with NGOs here, that they will always come on the victim, to ask these kinds of uncomfortable questions which should actually not be asked but are asked. And so, you have to take a fall if you want to go through it because it's like re-victimizing again, like going through the rape again.

MK

Correct, you go back to the incident in the mind.

Sujata

Exactly. Not just in the mind, but also in the physical setting. If day in day out you have to recount that, it is a very tough thing to do and it is something you have to be prepared for. It takes a lot of inner courage to take such a step. However, my advice always to the reader and audience is you must stand up because if you don't, you only perpetuate the crime to be committed more often. There's no stopping it. There's no stopping it even now. You shouldn't take it lying down.

MK

How does speaking out and fighting for things that have caused violation in a person's internal world, help in mental wellness and mental health?

Sujata

See, what happens if you bottle up things is that you're going to have all those sleepless nights. You're going to have all those nightmares, and you are going to feel very depressed and upset and you can't speak to anybody. So I'm saying even physically you will have all kinds of diseases because you're bottling it up. You think heart attacks, diabetes, blood pressure, happens just physically? If you ask any doctor, they will say the biggest reason for these diseases is stress. So where does the stress come from? But the only thing is, when you suffer from diabetes, a heart attack, or a high blood pressure kind of situation, there is no stigma attached. Whereas if you bottle up things and the mental aspect is mentioned, there is stigma attached. It is not treated the same way as diabetes, heart attack, or blood pressure.

So people will just say it's stress. They know the underlying cause, but they will not get into what caused the heart attack. They will probably say they were eating the wrong foods or not exercising. But rarely have I ever seen a doctor go into 'What is the stress level that caused you to have a heart attack?' People can look very healthy on the outside, but you will not know what battles they are fighting in their mental space, right? And that is what happens. So when you bottle it up, you're actually harming yourself more than the outside world. The outside world doesn't really matter because when you're going through it, does anybody come to your rescue? Nobody comes to your rescue.

MK

And the only person you can really rescue is yourself. And it starts from you wanting to help yourself.

Sujata

Yes, exactly. And why should you be in that position because of somebody else's actions? People forget that others' actions do affect us. We can see that others' actions or opinions do not define us. Just to give you an analogy: if I go out by the roadside and it starts raining, what do we do? We put on a raincoat, pull out an umbrella, or go into a shelter, right?

But if people are nasty to us, there is no such thing as actually protecting ourselves except by actually dealing with it. So it's not that we can protect ourselves by simply putting on a raincoat and becoming invincible as if people will not affect us. People can affect us and that is what human beings are all about. So if you don't want to speak out and you're only going to bottle up your baggages, then you have more processes to cure in a routine manner because looking after yourself and dealing with it is slightly unconventional. Most commonly we're taught to go to the doctor or a therapist or a counsellor and that has its own inhibitions, expectations, and repercussions.

MK

I'm hearing that the theme is really about standing up for yourself.

Sujata

Yes. You have to stand up for yourself first before you—

MK

Stand up for other people.

Sujata

You know when we're in the airplane, they say 'Put on your own oxygen mask before helping others'. It's the same thing. If you want to help others, you have to first help yourself. Only then can you help others. Writing the book was a healing process for me. Writing the book was inspirational because I could at least tell people who were sitting quietly, not knowing what to do, that this is what you can do at every stage and every step. It was not only that. My book has so many stories on how to deal with stalking, how to deal with bullying, or how to deal with harassment in various categories and stages.

MK

I was wondering . . . In terms of what you've seen out there, what can people do to help themselves to stand for themselves more?

Sujata

First and foremost, when an incident happens, whether it is minor or major, you need to step back. Don't rush immediately into a response or a reaction. First step back and observe the situation from an outside perspective.

The second thing is to accept that it happened. Let's not pretend it did not happen. Don't say 'You know, maybe I was at fault. Maybe I was mistaken. Maybe I deserved it'. Those are self-defeating beliefs that should not be there. Once you have accepted that it happened and understood that what happened was not your fault—if you were not responsible for it—then you work from there. If something bad happened to you, like you're walking down the street and you fall down and cut yourself, what will you do? You'll put a band-aid or disinfectant, or depending on the wound, go to the hospital, right? So in that kind of same procedure, you decide that this is something that you did not invite but has happened nonetheless, and you are going to deal with it. Once you decide that, it's a little easier for you to then see how you want to deal with it because you can't really take steps unless you know the context.

For example, it could be a situation in the office where somebody is harassing you. It could be a peer person or a supervisor. A peer or fellow colleague is a little bit easier to deal with because you're at an equal level, so you can use multiple techniques to give back, like using humour or by telling the person that you don't appreciate it. There are different methods. But if it's a supervisor, it's difficult because you might have to end up deciding if you need to leave your workplace. And if there's somebody higher than your immediate supervisor who you can walk to and make the complaint, then you should do that. Put it in writing. Always leave a trail record of every kind of wrongdoing because if you don't have that, you'll never get through it. The one thing I always say is 'Write it down and make it official'. Otherwise, it's your story versus my story and if somebody wants to say that you are bad in your head or making things up, there's no end to it. There will be people like that, even in their official capacity, who try to put you down. That's why people don't actually speak out, because the first response they might get is 'Oh you're overthinking. This didn't happen. Maybe you're imagining it. Or maybe it's your responsibility'.

So there are so many of these statements which will just make you go into your shell even if you take one step forward. But if you write down factually that on so-and-so date, this happened at so-and-so time, and you start keeping a journal of the situation, it's easier for higher-ups to go and take action because you'll be very firm and say 'This is what happened, this is the time it happened, this is how it happened'. Keep proof and evidence of everything. That's why I always advise: before you speak, think ten times. Before you write, think twenty times. Once written, you have to back up your words.

SETTING BOUNDARIES IS ABOUT SELF-RESPECT

MK

That is very very . . . you've been through a lot. There's a lot of wisdom to be unpacked in these life experiences. I was wondering if you could share a thing or two with people out there. What is the kind of society we can all work together to build? How can we build a community that stands for other people and more importantly, also sets boundaries? Because what you shared about paperwork is about creating boundaries so that things are set clearly in black and white, and nobody can create dramas out of it. Because when one person says one thing and another person says another thing, there's no end to it like you said. So it becomes a problem because what is the truth? How are we going to distinguish the truth? Because it's like hearsay. And we live in a social media age where people are so opinionated. Even if they don't know what the hell they're talking about, people—

Sujata

Have to say something!

MK

And they start getting swayed by opinions rather than facts. So I like what you said about setting things black and white, because it's all about setting boundaries. Do you have anything you want to comment about boundaries?

Sujata

So how I operate is I follow Richard Feynman's—

MK

Richard Feynman!

Sujata

Yes. Richard Feynman's way of operating was that you observe, and then you experiment, and then come to a conclusion. So you don't just blindly believe everything that is taught to you, and you question everything and experiment everything to find out *does this work or does this not work?* Then you come to a conclusion on how you can deal with it. It's actually very simple but we humans make it tough. If we are a little bit kind—now, kindness is not taught—but if we are kind and we don't judge, I say that the good and bad is within us. People talk of God. I always say God and the Devil are within us. It is always through our actions. We don't look at a person, we look at their actions, because through their actions you will know them. So you know, people talk of love and all that. But if the love does not have respect, that love is going to be flawed. When we talk about boundaries, always remember one thing—that no matter what the relationship is, you have to have self-respect. If you have self-respect, you also respect others. Then you are very clear that this is one line people don't cross.

So it's okay that we have different views and approaches to doing things. But when it comes to self-respect, that is a boundary we do not cross because that's when you invade my space and when you do that, you're attacking me, or you're being a threat to somebody's peace of mind. Or if it's physical, then it's physical safety. So you must have the self-respect so that the moment you see something which doesn't feel right, which your gut instinct will tell you, you can say no. It doesn't matter who it is. It could be a parent, could be a spouse, could be a child, but you should say 'No, this is wrong'. So you cannot generalize right easily, but you can always generalize the wrong. You can define your boundaries easily, and once you define them, then you can clearly deal with the wrong.

MK

Sometimes we have to say no to things so that we can say yes to the important things in life.

Sujata

Yes, exactly! So you have to say no. And if you have to say no, then you have to say no, no matter who it is. You see, because of titles and designations, we tend to say yes even when we want to say no. And that's where we lose the boundary. It gets diluted.

MK

And sometimes we violate our internal self, internal world, value system, and principles because we say yes to the things we know we shouldn't have said yes to. Part of the game is learning to say no, and part of that is about growing up.

Sujata

And you constantly evolve, by the way. There is no limit to your growing and evolving. So you grow and evolve at every stage of life because at every stage you will encounter different kinds of situations and experiences that are not what you experience when you're a child or adolescent. So you still should maintain that self-respect and self-care. And it's not about words alone. What I'm trying to say is, we need to carry out all this in action. Like you said, social media. Social media is all about words and visuals. It doesn't have the authenticity or the genuineness of the person is not reflected. All you see are pictures. You can modify a picture with photoshop, or with social media or whatever. You have all the tools to make. But do you know the person? Do you *actually* know the person?

MK

Do you really know what is real and what is not? What is the truth?

Sujata

And what are they leading their lives towards apart from what they're showing you that they're doing? What are they doing behind closed doors? You'll never know what's happening behind closed doors because not everybody is an open book. Remember that. Most people, 99 per cent of the population, have a facade. One for the outside world and one for the inside. So you have to be aware. And if you have empathy and can pick out from your surroundings and see that there's something wrong, you can try to reach out and say 'is everything okay?' Sometimes it just takes that little bit of care for somebody to open up, who might be going through a challenging time on their own. We don't do that. We also think, if somebody's going through a challenge, that we should give them space. Why would you want space to be alone? You would want some care and love and affection. This is something I don't understand. There are people I know who have this kind of attitude. I believe that if you're going through something, reach out. Reach out to a person who is willing to be there for you. That is me. If you find somebody good and proper, great. If you don't, then you have to rely on your inner courage.

WHAT LIES BEHIND SUICIDE?

Sujata

So when we talk about suicide, here is my take on it. Why do people commit suicide? The perception is that people are cowards. But it's not really because you're a coward. There's so many aspects to it. Take for example the famous cases of celebrity suicides. They have all the money in the world. They have friends, they have families, and they have access to all kinds of therapists and counsellors. Why do they still commit suicide? Because whatever they're suffering from—the loneliness, or the pressure of the industry, or whatever they're going through— they find themselves alone. So that's what happens when you find yourself alone and unable to find somebody who would help you.

It's a known fact that suicides have been averted if that person found, just at that moment, somebody to talk to. And if that person talks for an hour or two with real empathy and understanding, you can change the mind of the person and stop them from taking that drastic action. But in many cases, it's not there and people in those positions actually lead a very lonely life. That's why you'll see a lot of celebrity suicides all over the world. Like the Robin Williams case. He lived in a mansion, he had everything going right. Why did he commit suicide? Why did nobody ever understand what he was going through? Perhaps the people surrounding you are not caring enough to see the signs. There are always some signs that you can perceive if somebody's unhappy. But if you don't take action on it, then the person will probably end up taking drastic actions. It's not a question of being a coward. It actually takes a lot of courage to commit suicide, I feel.

Another thing I wanted to question is meditation. That is a very loose term. If you're in a war zone, especially for countries who have had border fights going on for years, how do the people live there? Can you tell them that when you're in the bomb shelter, you just sit, close your eyes, and meditate? It's not so easy. What if somebody's lost their job, they're living pay check to pay check, and they've a family to support? You think it's easy? To just close your eyes and meditate? No. So you have to find ways of actually being in the situation and dealing with yourself. It's not easy. But there are tools and techniques to help you. But the major thing is to accept the situation. If you accept the situation, you say 'Okay, what can I do?' You put it down clearly, 'These are the things I can do or cannot do'.

And give yourself time to breathe and heal. That's another thing we don't do. We are always prone to telling people, 'I'm sorry for your loss, but move on'. It's like when a death happens, we go through a ritual of twelve days, thirteen days, or four days, or five days—according to your society or culture. Once we finish with that it's as if we're supposed to forget that it happened. You think people will forget mourning or grieving for their loss because their rituals have finished? It doesn't happen that way! So you must understand when somebody's going through this and allow this person to breathe. Just say 'I'm there for you'. And instead of telling them don't cry or their crying or mourning period is over, encourage people to cry, because crying is very cleansing and healing. There's a reason why we are attuned to crying. So we should not stop ourselves from crying. That's an emotional expression. So you should allow that. Everything is of course contextual, we are not going to associate one type of crying with the other, like a baby throwing a tantrum for a toy. But regarding grieving and mourning, crying should be encouraged and not repressed or discouraged from happening. And it's not gender-specific, I feel.

MK

Thank you. I thought it was very insightful and wise.

Sujata

It is my pleasure to contribute on this topic. This is a topic I'm very close to, and a topic which affects all of us. It's not that we are any different. It doesn't matter which part of the globe we're in, what is our colour, what is our creed—it doesn't matter. All of the things we're talking about affect all of us. Some more, some less. Some may have cultural connotations which may not be present in other parts of the world, but the fact remains that trauma is trauma and tragedy is tragedy. And this is the biggest tutor in learning. It can shape your character, or it can break you, if you buckle under it.

CHAPTER FOUR

If We Take Care of Each Other, We Benefit Collectively

By Charlotte Goh, Executive Director, Playeum Ltd

Charlotte's eating disorder began twenty years ago. Because of her Tourette's syndrome, she always felt that she was not good enough. As a result, binging and smoking became her coping mechanisms. Charlotte reflects on her journey to recovery, and the AHA! moments she experienced that really consolidated change within her. As a director of a social service agency, she had to grapple with potentially closing her agency due to COVID-19, and how she is dealing with that by relying on the wisdom she has built up over the years of healing.

MY JOURNEY WITH MY EATING DISORDER AND SMOKING

Charlotte

My eating disorder started twenty years ago. I was not an easy child. Because of my Tourette syndrome, from young, even though it's probably not true, the different dynamics between my brother, myself and my parents left me with the feeling that I was not good enough.

MK

'I'm not good enough.'

Charlotte

Yeah, 'I'm not good enough'. So I was always the not good enough one. I always overcompensated and I depended a lot on external validation, be it from parents, teachers, partners, or work. And my coping mechanisms for those last twenty years was to smoke, binge and throw up.

Looking back, I was on this mouse wheel, constantly running towards something, running towards a bigger achievement, a bigger project, something better. I was seeking that validation, and the bigger the validation, the better I felt.

The inner work started when I became bulimia-free. It was very strange. It was actually because my very good friend and I were having a massage in Lombok and for some years I was trying to get pregnant. And whilst we were having a massage, she said oh my god, I realized why you can't get pregnant! I was like why? And she said because you keep throwing up!

I was throwing up at least six times a day. When she said that, I had this vision in my mind that the violent force of contracting was not going to hold the pregnancy. It was as though every time you try to hold the pregnancy, the baby wants to latch right but urrrgh it's so stressful, how can the baby latch? And from that moment onwards, I just stopped throwing up!

But it took years of help that I sought at IMH. I had counsellors when I was studying in Australia, social workers helping me in the past. But honestly that's the thing right, why didn't all that help work? I had questioned counselling. Why didn't it help? Counselling takes years, right? I now understand that to truly heal, it takes work within yourself, and that means that all the years of counselling added up to that one day. What my friend said was a trigger that jolted me.

MK

It clicked.

Charlotte

We decided to do IVF the following year. Our son was born through IVF and I was like well if I'm doing IVF, I should seriously stop smoking right? It had been really tough to stop previously. I tried acupuncture, I tried the patches, I tried hypnosis, whatever. All the things that were supposed to help you, I tried. And finally I found out about the Allen Carr programme from a friend. So there was a money-back guarantee, where you pay X amount of money and after the programme, which is half a day, if you don't decide to stop smoking, you get your money back. But I wanted to stop smoking, and I did!

I gave birth to Jonas at forty, so quite late. Somehow in that same year, the opportunity came up to explore EFT[3], which is tapping. It's sold to you as a way to alleviate your problems or get into a better state. But of course, what I didn't realize is that it unearths a lot of stuff in your life. It unearths all your anger, your guilt, your I'm not good enough, the Pandora's box that you never wanted to open. So that started my deeper inner work journey. I'm fifty this year, so it's been ten years. I'm in a much better

---

[3] EFT: Emotional Freedom Technique

space. I am still doing the work with different coaches. I don't think it ever ends. We just evolve. Once you see, you can't unsee.

HOW DO YOU SCALE UP TRUST AND RELATIONSHIPS?

Charlotte

Sometimes I grapple with the social sector work which we're in, because you realize a lot of the work is built on trust and relationships, and how do you scale up trust and relationships? And that's so powerful because the work we do with any child or any adult can be a one-time intervention or a period of intervention, but if you really want to see change you got to journey with people—at least for a while. Trust. How do you scale that up? When grant makers invest, many invest in scaling up. I know it's possible to scale up programmes but what about transformation?

MK

It's like that. We're going down the rabbit hole.

Charlotte

I don't know whether you would call it a rabbit hole. All these programmes are great, they can help people. I think the true work starts within, and starts with being aware of it. But not everyone's ready for it. I know that because looking inside your Pandora's box is not easy. Unearthing it and facing it is even harder.

When I was twenty-six, I remember sitting on a swing with a guy I used to have a crush on. And I was telling him that I don't want to open the Pandora's box. When he asked me what was going on in my mind, I said I don't want to talk about it. I remember sitting on that swing, and it was crazy because I was about to tear up just thinking about looking deeper. It was so heavy, I didn't want to deal with it, so I pushed it aside until I was forty. And that was interesting because I don't think I suffered, but it was a façade.

It was a mask. I appeared to be very confident on the outside, but the truth was, I was crumbling inside and not seeing that I was.

I started the first eating disorder support group with a doctor from IMH and two sufferers. I remember chairing or hosting those meetings with her and the team and I was still going through it myself then, and I had to put on a mask for everyone because you are hosting. Of course, people knew I was still struggling with it and that I was better but not totally there yet. But after a while I gave up because it was too much of a burden to put up a braver front. It's a lot, it's a burden, it's heavy, and to hold secrets is heavy. So even with my friends, only a handful spoke to me about it. So many people did not dare broach the topic even though they knew I was going through this. I always think to myself, if I cared enough for anyone, whether it's an eating disorder or just not exercising enough or whether you're overweight to the point of unhealthiness or you're doing things that harm yourself, do I care enough to tell the person? Or even if you're not aware and you're doing silly things that make you look embarrassing in front of people, should I tell you? Right? I mean if I care enough about you, I should, but I think to myself is the person ready to hear it? If they are not, am I prepared to deal with the aftermath?

MK

It's a constant struggle. Is the person ready for the truth? Because the truth can break a person if they're not ready. You need the sensitivity, the intuition, the time and space.

Charlotte

If our time and space align, certain conversations will emerge.

So I learnt something from someone recently and he shared with me the importance about being patient and waiting for the right time. It's a bit like the minute my husband comes home, I just download my entire day to my husband and he's like freaking out you know. Especially some guys are like oh my god can you not bombard me with all these stories? They just need to calm down, right? It's really about time and space. Then you quarrel because 'Oh you never want to listen to my stories, I'm not important enough', but of course it's not true. It's the time and space.

Even if it's addressing a concern I have with someone, I am starting to think about being patient for the right time and space. If I rush to get it out of my system, is that for me, or truly for the person? It's a question I think about. And sometimes, yes, maybe the need to speak is for me. I even start asking permission like would you mind if I shared something with you? Sometimes articulating what I need from the person like I just need you to listen, I need some advice because then you set the context for your next download, you know what I mean?
[laughter]

JUST GO FOR IT

Charlotte

So yeah. Where were we? What are we talking about?

MK

Well, we're talking about fundamental responsibility, we're talking about whether the person is ready to hear the truth, which is an important factor when it comes to mental health.

Charlotte

So I think the last time I felt really down and out and depressed was when I was in university. I think I'm a very hard worker. I got straight As only because of my hard work. I mean look at our A levels. You can, if you study and memorize everything, get straight As at that time. So I was a mugger because I had a lot to prove to myself. So I got straight As, got into the course I wanted in university. I always wanted to go to that university, it was like my dream come true.

MK

I have the exact same story, so when you're talking it feels like you're a parallel of me.

Charlotte

Yeah so I got in and I was so disappointed with the culture because I came from a convent school where everyone was so caring, we would share notes and everything but I was just really surprised at how different things were in university and I just felt miserable back then. I cried everyday, I didn't want to go to school. Then my father said 'So what do you want to do?' I said 'I want to join the army'. Then he said the best thing he could say. 'Then go for it, go for it'. And I think that choice and agency my father gave me was powerful. It made me think about what I wanted to do but it also made me realize that I do want to study at university, just not here.

So I applied for a grant on the third interview, I said 'Yeah I really want to get into WOCS,[4] I want to go into infantry'. I don't know why I wanted that because honestly, I don't even dare to shoot anyone right now, what made me think I could join the army? So maybe the universe knew but what turned me off was the fact that I would have to work as an admin staff rather than the infantry. I asked him 'Why?' and the interviewer said 'Because you're a woman'. And I was like what? But that was quite some time ago, thirty years to be exact. Thank God we have progressed.

I came from a family where I felt that my brother was more favoured and now it's repeating itself. I was so for gender equality because I felt it was very unfair already at home, although it was probably not true, but it was my lens. And so I didn't join the army and I decided okay I'm going to work then. So I applied for university in Australia, and whilst I was waiting for the application

---

[4] WOCS: Warrant Officer Cadet School

status I started working in all kinds of jobs. I sold heating packs at pharmacies. I did graphic design too and I did well because my father's an artist and my brother's an architect, so somehow it runs in the family. But graphic design wasn't my thing, so I decided to go and sell the heat packs because I had 1 per cent commission on every one I sold so I sold a hell of a lot of it. [laughter]

Charlotte

At that time, there were no emails, no computers still. The Australian government was afraid to take me in because of my Tourette syndrome. So they wrote to me through snail mail asking me questions about my Tourette. One month later, another mail would come, another question. They were afraid that I would depend on their welfare state but I had no intention of doing that. I mean, I'm the sort that would not depend on people to pay for me. I would work. So I managed to prove it to them, finally one and a half years later, I got into Australia.

MK

One and a half years later!

Charlotte

About there. So that was my journey to university. I was miserable and in a depressive state then. In that depressive state, you're clouded in your mind, you're not clear, but what gave me that option and that freedom was my dad telling me to 'Do what you want'. I didn't have the pressure of having to complete what I'm supposed to complete by a certain time, which was everybody's path right? Go to O levels, A levels, university, get married, you know all these paths that our society expects of us. So that gave me a lot of freedom, to have options. I think to know that I had an option was like wow, suddenly my mind was not cloudy anymore. And suddenly my energy went all out into exploring my options.

Then the second time I felt down was honestly during COVID, but it was not depression, it was probably melancholy. I had to make big decisions about the charity, and I felt that we had to close the centre. It was a very big decision that I think no one person individually wanted to make, but me being the executive director, had to call it and after a while it became very clear that if we didn't close the centre within four months we'll shut. I made that decision, but I also had strong support from the board. They encouraged me, they supported me, they guided me but I think the decision had to come from my mouth. So to say it was almost therapeutic in releasing, but fearful too.

MK

What did it take for you to speak it out?

Charlotte

I think there was a lot of uncertainty and what helped me was actually walking in nature because I was stuck working in these four walls. And it was COVID lockdown right, this state of melancholy was heavy. I'll use the word melancholic. Depression's different. I've been depressed so I think this is not. It helps that I have lived experiences with depression and eating disorders in the past, so I knew how to recognize the signs that something might be brewing inside me. It's important for people to learn how to recognize these signs.

So anyway I grappled with it. Like you could see I was on the verge of being like okay if I don't take care of myself, this is what it's like to have a mental condition, oh my god this is what it feels like. You could see that I was on the verge of it. So I went into nature a lot and I walked it out. What helped me was to be vulnerable and to admit that.

I didn't know what I needed to do and I asked people who I trusted for advice. I shared with them what was going on and there were two very senior and experienced people who advised me. I turned to them, I laid all my financials out, and you have to be vulnerable, don't have the ego to say you know when you don't. And that helped me have more clarity. So clarity unclouds the mind. Clarity on what I needed to do next lifted that 'not knowing-ness' and it uplifted my spirits. Then I did the math, the staff salaries, my monthly costs, how much I needed, everything. And that gave me clarity and things made so much more sense.

Now the question is where do I play, how do I play, and who do I play with? It's that sweet spot to play for impact but yet be sustainable. So I am festering in uncertainty but I'm also embracing uncertainty. It doesn't scare me, because I think the direction we're heading is a direction I'm very happy with. It's a question of greatest impact and sustainability now. I don't fear the outcome and if we have to close in one year, okay, we've done our part. We've been here eleven, twelve years, so we've done our part. So I don't fear the worst outcome. There is a Buddhist saying that attachment brings suffering, which is very true. Because you're so attached to the outcome, I must succeed, or I must have this, I must have that, that you fear losing it or fear not getting it and that brings suffering. So I'm not attached to it, but I do my best. And I mean of course if we close we'll all be out of a job, we all have finances to pay, but I always trust that something will always come along for us and our team. So I have a huge trust in the universe and a huge trust in God.

So yeah. These are the two periods I noticed a slide in my mental health. But the second time during COVID, I was really aware of it. So I went to do something about it. I gave myself more clarity that would uplift myself. I went into nature and even took up mountain biking. It's very healing.

I also realized that again it's the space you come from. I think being open, honest and vulnerable enough is very important. I'm going to use the word ego, but I don't mean ego in a bad way. Ego puts a barrier. So having humility helps, especially when you don't know a lot of things other than your area of expertise, and even with that, there is so much more to grow. So I realized that the values that helped me were vulnerability, humility, being, especially being present in the moment, being self-aware. In order for a person to trust me, I need to trust first and I think when you trust first, it opens a lot of floodgates for more love to come. People are more willing to open their hearts to you and I think that's when there's a trusting dynamic between interpersonal relationships. The speed of productivity or whatever you want to call it goes faster. And that all lifts you up somehow, you see.

THE IMPORTANCE OF VOICE AND AGENCY

MK

Got it. So you talked about finding solutions out of the challenges we face. There are a lot of themes that keep coming up. What do you think is stopping people from seeking help? Because from my understanding, a lot of times we don't have the ability to distinguish whether we're experiencing mental health, mental wellness, or even mental illness. There's a lack of awareness about mental health.

Charlotte

I think people seek help when they want to end suffering. But if you don't know that you're sliding or slipping down, then you need a community of people around you to be aware to say that hey babe, you need some help. And then it introduces the idea that oh I have an option. That's why I think coaching is important. I don't use the word coaching because people always think that everyone is a coach, why would I hire a coach? It's not a coach, it's people to scaffold your growth. Coaches push you beyond, they push you enough to go beyond your limiting beliefs but not enough for you to give up. Friends can do this too. But it takes a community around you to be aware that something's happening to this person and someone to say hey do you need help? Are you okay?

Sometimes, we are not the ones who can help but we can introduce them to other resources. Many of my friends ask me for recommendations for their conditions whether it's stress, marital problems, or issues with children. But I myself don't know enough resources to recommend. So I'll go to my friends in the social sector and seek resources from the community.

But I do think it takes people in the community to be aware of someone sliding. We cannot be apathetic or indifferent to people we care about. A lot of times in Singaporean culture, we can be very scared of bringing out confrontational issues. We're not good with confrontation. Even I myself don't like confrontations, but I will bring up things especially if I need to make it better. But we're not good at that. We don't want to talk about things. It's just our culture. First and foremost, voice and agency is not a very big thing for us in Singapore. That's why Playeum is trying to give opportunities for voice and agency in children. But I also think it's important to exercise responsibility when we have a voice, you know what I mean?

I think it's a balance. If people don't have a voice right, it gets stuck. It's quite a suffering to hold back thoughts and ideas that you can't voice out. For example, I went for a workshop recently and I have Tourette. At one point I started ticcing a lot, but no one asked me about it and I did not have the chance to tell anyone in this room of twenty-eight people. I felt like the white elephant in the room, even though I'm comfortable with my tics. I felt like everyone noticed but nobody wanted to talk about it. So during one of the sessions, I just put up my hand and said guys, I got to say something to you. I have Tourette, I have tics, just don't worry about it. As I was saying it right, I teared up. And I didn't expect that because I'm over it, I can cope with it, but I was emotional about having a voice. Nobody asked me about it, and I didn't need people to, I just needed to voice it out cause once you know I have it right, you will just ignore it like oh that's just Charlotte.

Give you another example. In the lift, if I'm ticcing away, and I say oh sorry I have a nerve problem, suddenly people are like oh don't worry about it, my friend has that too and suddenly the tension dissipates, or what I perceive as tension. But if I'm in a lift and I'm ticcing a lot and people are like oh my god what's wrong with her? Awkkkkwarrd!! It's this silence that's heavy with tension. I know the power of putting yourself in that position to voice it and it helps! It eases attention for me at least, so I know how to go about my lift survival techniques!

It's the power of voice, having to speak up, like the LGBTQ+ issue. The reason why it's becoming more and more prominent is because we haven't given it a proper voice and it's building up because the voice is not fully heard. It's been shut down so many times, and it will become something to deal with very soon because the voice is getting louder. Does it make sense?

MK

It does.

Charlotte

When people do not have a voice, they feel stifled. They suffer because it's like being in a pressure cooker. Pink Dot is growing because it's a voice for many who don't have a voice.

MK

We're talking about collective suppression over the years and its reaction force.

Charlotte

Yes, yes! And I'm not saying whether it's right or wrong but people need platforms and opportunities to voice out. There's no moral judgement, it's just that people who are going through certain things need a voice. With mental health, I think what would help is the community stepping up to not be apathetic or indifferent to recognizing signs. You know we're a collective energy. It's not Charlotte in silos. It's not MK in silos. We're all from the same source, we're collective energies. If we start taking care of each other, collectively we all benefit.

MK

We are taking care of ourselves.

Charlotte

Yeah, we all benefit. So if we start being less apathetic and indifferent to our friends and family around us, even foes honestly, because sometimes foes are foes because they have their own problems; we can all benefit. That's why this *kampong*[5] spirit is something I really I mean it's cliché but it's very powerful when you look out for each other because we are a collective spirit, that's how I see it. So looking out for others, noticing it yourself, also means the community noticing it.

Another thing about mental health is when the person cannot 'see', the collective spirit needs to see and help them. That's how

---

[5] Kampong: Traditional village

I think we can make a difference. It's really ideal if we're brave enough to care. But I must say our politics are getting a bit more interesting, people are getting less apathetic. At one point fewer people were inclined towards politics because it was all walkovers, remember? So funny right. But over the years, and as we've seen in the last election, people are not so apathetic and indifferent anymore. They are more passionate about what they want to see in Singapore. There's no good or bad, it's just how it is. The fact is that I saw a lot more people interested in our welfare, especially in who runs our country, to me is a positive sign. I see more voices emerging. I find that it's a very flourishing and thriving space.

THE NATIONAL SERVICE FOR MENTAL HEALTH

MK

Well what do you think, you know . . . This question is a little bit hard because I didn't plan to ask this in this conversation. What do you think we can do from an individual level to a collective level or even from the policy level?

Charlotte

You know, there was something I wanted to share with you, a simple example.

During my army craze when I wanted to go to the army right, I wrote into a forum when I was sixteen asking why women couldn't go serve National Service. And my idea of National Service was not to run around for two years with a gun. I thought women should learn at least about first aid, about how to be first responders. Like if our army boys come back injured, can we administer first aid? Can we cook meals from nothing, can we build from nothing, can we make something? Fine, send them to hold a gun, launch a missile, but women can contribute too. We're born nurturers. So I feel that if you have this National Service concept of serving the nation, what would serve the nation is empowering citizens with certain skills as first responders for mental health.

We may not be qualified to counsel someone all the way, but being a first responder is about when you notice a sign, what can you say, how can you react, how can you help? I think that's National Service, isn't it? It's not always about external security, it's internal security too. Maybe we don't have to go for a two-year course but two months? Three months? Why not? First responder course, you know. Okay lah nowadays no time, everyone's rushing to get academics done but I feel this whole idea of National Service is to serve our nation. To serve our community. To serve ourselves.

National Service should be for all the citizens. I think head knowledge is one thing that's important but it's more than head it's heart knowledge as well.

MK

You see the problem is we are not trained on how to use our heart. We've been trained in school to use our brain to think, I hope, but we were never taught to listen to our heart. We don't understand the language of the heart, we don't understand the logic of the heart.

Charlotte

To be fair there are some very good programmes like what The Thought Collective delivers. Seriously, we got to start people thinking about the work they do with themselves, if they want to go out there and start living lives to be whole human beings as a collective nation. It's very powerful to start young because there's less work to undo. That's why we do National Service young because we're fitter, we're more flexible. So the concept of National Service to me at the policy level is what content goes into National Service and who you involve. Equipping everyone with the skills to be first responders is going to be very powerful because when you've done a course, you would also start noticing things about your own mental wellbeing like oh god I think I'm slipping at some stage. And if you're not aware, say if you're cutting yourself or you're hurting yourself, if there's enough conversation and voice around this topic and people are not afraid to speak up, then people could reach out to you and you can get help. Like nobody asked me about my eating disorder except honestly two of my friends who were close to me. My husband addressed it with me and the fact that he loved me unconditionally despite all this was probably part of the healing. So then the healing started and I knew that I didn't have to be someone I'm not. I could strip the doing of the throwing up and just be who I am. So because my relationship was supportive, I could heal. So whether it's your parents, or whether it's your other family members, friends or whether it's community, I think if you have that support it does help to heal. It can help. How do we build policy? I would say think about what National Service really means to the nation, and else goes into that content.

I also think the more voice this topic is given, the less people feel fearful of addressing it. If you remove the difficultness of the conversation, things ease up and people are more willing to talk about it and it becomes not so painful, not so taboo to talk about it and not so taboo to seek help. You know all my friends who are somewhat close with me shared in their lifetime that they've gone through a period of somewhat depression and a lot of it happened or started in their teens and twenties, because growing up is hard. In my younger days I had growing up issues, I had an eating disorder, I had Tourette syndrome, and it's just not an easy time. And so I realize that many come out of it, but some don't, or some make choices that are harmful long-term.

My father was the one that released that pain from me by giving me an option, a way out. I think a lot of people with mental health issues don't think there's a way out or can't see it yet because they're clouded. Their struggle with the mental health issue clouds the brain. From my experience, I didn't know why I did the things I did. It didn't matter even if I did something that was not right. I didn't have a clear mind, as if I was on some mind-numbing state.

COMING FROM A SPACE OF LOVE

MK

I totally get what you're saying. Now, if there's something that you would like the world to know about mental health, mental wellness, their own journey, whether it is inner work or even the external journey itself, what would it be?

Charlotte

Relationships are very important to me, especially quality relationships. Not the number of people you have but the number of quality relationships you have. We don't exist alone and I do feel that. It sounds like I must say some big profound thing. But if I strip off those expectations, I think for me, the most important thing to start with is self-awareness. Who am I and what space do I come from? So for example, if I react versus I respond, what space is that? I tend to want to operate out of a, I know it sounds very cliché, but out of a space of love. When I say love, I don't mean romantic love, but it's a love for a fellow human being. It's love for yourself because your self is manifested in everything in this world. We're all energy beings from the same source, I believe. We're just masked differently. You have this mask and I have this mask, that's all. I can actually at some stage strip you of your gender and see you as another energy being. If I need to, I can. I don't see you as a man, a woman or whatever gender you identify with. Some energy beings are in pain, some are more liberated. That's why I think that being aware of what I bring to the table is important. When I say I act out of love, I mean love for my own self, my own energy being, my own source. You understand?

MK

I do.

Charlotte

So anyway, I think that the most important thing is if we can have more self-awareness, because it starts with self. I think a lot of relationships that you enjoy, at the end of the day, are out of a pursuit of happiness. At a very basic level, we all pursue happiness or joy. Whether you're poor or rich, educated or uneducated, whatever, all the choices we make are about people and things that bless us, bring us joy, fill us, complete us. It starts with yourself. Are you happy with yourself, do you like yourself? Because even if people love you and take care of you, if you're not happy with yourself, you will suffer. So it starts with self-awareness. Our relationships with ourselves.

CHAPTER FIVE

Self-Discovery in Everything You Do

By Lynette Xia (Har), Life Transition Coach and Strategist

As a coach working with women, executives or entrepreneurs, Lynette talks about the challenges around being present in a busy world. We all juggle multiple roles in life, so it is important to pause and ask ourselves why we do what we do, and embark on a journey of self-discovery to uncover what it is that truly matters to us.

VALUE SYSTEMS STRENGTHEN OUR CORE

MK

Lynette, why don't you share with me a little bit about what you do as a coach?

Lynette

I was in corporate for fifteen to sixteen years doing account servicing, but for personal reasons, I decided to leave at the peak of my career. So it's been a journey of discovery ever since. Because the part about maximizing one's potential, being able to manage the stresses of the everyday . . . It's a process. Once you're able to manage yourself, you're able then to give back. I see that process happening in my clients as well. That's why it's so beautiful, and that's why I'm so addicted to this new profession, this second phase of my life. I am a Life Coach who will work with you in a collaborative and empowering journey together to create stalwart transitions across your professional and personal life, whilst holding space for what matters of the heart. I am a certified Peak Performance Coach with the International Coaching Federation (ICF) and am working towards my Professional Coaching Certification (PCC) accreditation.

The clients that typically come to me are women, executives, or entrepreneurs who are stuck, who have been frustrated with themselves and the work they do on a personal front and on a family front as well for the longest time. I see the constant struggle between work, family, and self. It is a vicious cycle. Many want to be better but struggle with the multiple roles they have. The mummy guilt. They are often torn apart between obligations, responsibilities and their own needs. Because they are unable to see the light, they become frustrated with themselves, angry with those around them, often lashing at those closest to them without actually meaning to, only to regret after the 'fight' and try to make things up with material things. Some cope, some don't. But they want to see a change in themselves and get better at what they are doing. I help them get unstuck and with the breakthroughs that they have, the amount of joy that they have brought not only to themselves, but also to the family is amazing. And that has a ripple effect down to the children because they are our future generation. If we're able to impact that change from the source, I think it's great fulfilment. It's not therapy!

MK

It's not therapy! Coaching is not therapy.

Lynette

It's not therapy, and there is a misconception out there in the market as well

MK

Really? [In disbelief] Still?

Lynette

Yes, there is, there is. And it's so stereotypical but it's not therapy. I'm not a therapist. So it's a process of education as well.

The other thing is that, and I don't know if it's just in Singapore, but it's always tell me what I should do. But if I tell you what you should do, it's something that I would do, not what you would do, so it defeats the purpose.

MK

Yeah, correct, because it's not you. And coaching allows a person to get closer to their inner truth, the core of who they are, so that they can pursue what really matters to them, whatever that is.

Lynette

Correct! And it's a bit like with what you said, the core of who they are, but we call it peeling the onions, right? Getting to know your belief system; the values and beliefs that drive your decisions. Not many people are actually aware of that. It's about this discovery of the self, which I went through as well in my coaching journey. It's a mind-blowing experience.

MK

How does knowing your value system allow a person to strengthen the core of their mental and emotional health?

Lynette

The first thought that comes to mind is personality tools, because there are so many personality tools out there, right? And they classify or group you into categories. But what is different is that all our value systems, the environment that we were brought up in, the family that we stayed with, are different. So when you get through to each person beyond what's bothering them on the surface, you realize that it's got a deeper-rooted issue in their values, in their belief system, and that brings about new awareness. Once you have mental awareness, once you're consciously aware of what you're thinking of, it then drives that behaviour, that action, and then it creates a ripple effect. So that's why I think connecting with yourself is so important! And that's where that self-care or self-love comes back [laughter].

MK

When you go online these days, you see many people talking about self-love and self-care. But what does it really mean to love yourself? What does it really mean to care about yourself? What do you think?

Lynette

For me, it is time set aside for myself because as a mum-preneur, which is what I call myself, I have to manage both sides—my responsibilities and self. Women, regardless of the country or shape that we are in, have to manage multiple roles and find the sweet spot in between for that precious me-time. It's rare. So in my journey, it's been about four to five years now since I've left corporate, I found that my exercise time is my me-time, and that is so critical, so precious to me. Because when I have that me-time, I reflect and I go deep down into why am I thinking the way I am thinking? It helps me reflect, calibrate, and I intentionally set time for it. The key word here is to intentionally set time aside for activities that mean something. And if I don't do that, I can't fulfil the other obligations in my life 100 per cent. And I want to be 100 per cent. It's a choice that I make. Without that, the rest cannot go on!

ALWAYS GO BACK TO YOUR 'WHY'

MK

It's interesting that you talked about being intentional. How can individuals be more intentional in their day-to-day life so that they're ready to take on more?

Lynette

It comes back to why are you doing what you're doing? The first layer that a lot of my clients go through is the 'what'. What are you doing? Once they're able to discover that, then we go and figure out 'why' they are doing that. Then they realize that some of the things they're doing actually do not tie in with why they're doing what they're doing. When they realize that there is a disconnect, that's when the aha! moment happens. They realize that for example, hey, I'm spending ten hours of my time at work because I need to pay the bills for my family. But when you're at a certain stage of your career and your salary is sufficiently able to cover family expenses, why are you still doing that extra hour? Why? And if you're able to answer that question, you're answering to yourself in that process, and you discover what's happening within. And you start discovering hey, maybe I'm not spending my time on what's really important to me. That's what I mean by setting intentional time aside, because in the fast-paced society that we live in today, there's a lot of 'noise' in our environment. There are a lot of distractions. And there's a fear of judgement, which is where stigma comes from as well. People are doing things for the sake of others, or for the sake of doing something. Why does it matter, and does it really matter to you? And if it doesn't, are you going to take a stand for it? You have a choice to make.

MK

A lot of times, we get so caught up in doing that we forget the original intention of why we do what we do in the first place. And when that happens, people become very mechanical. And sometimes I think it takes, besides intention, a lot of intentional *awareness* to be able to catch yourself that hey, actually what I'm doing doesn't lead me to the place that I want to be.

Lynette

Correct. But before you can come to that realization, you need to spend time with yourself. If you don't spend time with yourself . . . Okay, those courses are not going to like me when I say this, but no matter how many courses that you go for—

MK

Or watching those motivational videos, it doesn't work!

Lynette

Yeah! It's just not going to sink in. You can attend a course and find out that oh maybe this is what I want to do. But what are you going to do about it? If you haven't owned that knowledge, if you haven't internalized it, you're going to go back into that same cycle. And that's where people are constantly stuck, which is actually quite sad.

SHOWING UP IN YOUR LIFE

MK

How can individuals start building a stronger, greater, and deeper awareness so that they have the ability to really catch themselves? I'm not talking about mindfulness, I'm talking about awareness.

Lynette

Yes, because they're different. They're actually quite distinctly different. [laughing] What is your definition of mindfulness?

MK

My definition of mindfulness is . . . If consciousness is passive, awareness is active, and mindfulness is the act of practicing that awareness. That's my definition.

Lynette

It's the act of practicing that awareness consciously on a daily basis—or if I can say, even on a microsecond basis—that allows you to have a breakthrough on another level. It is being aware of your actions, what you are putting out there be it for others or for yourself, the way that you're showing up for that minute or that second. Because our actions are a result of what's happening in the millions of internal voices that are going through us.

MK

And a lot of times, people don't realize that all these little internal voices are also one of the many factors influencing our mental health and our emotional wellness. Many people don't see the connection because we are too disconnected from ourselves and we don't have a deep understanding of ourselves.

Lynette

Yeah, correct, which is so sad. And I think a lot has to do with the world that we're living in. Look at digitalization, look at technology, look at the way information is flowing through! In the past when we did not have mobile phones, when you couldn't instantly connect with a person, it gave you time to process. But now when you meet online, it's so easy to zoom from one place to another, and I'm guilty of that, having back-to-back meetings without giving yourself that time and space to just internalize, sink in, and digest before you go into the next meeting. People don't give themselves that time anymore because they don't realize the damage that they're doing, not only to themselves, but to the people who are around them—you know as I'm saying that, my goosebumps are rising, because I see that happening with my clients. And it's so so sad. My heart breaks, actually, for the families because of the repercussions that the family goes through.

MK

It doesn't just affect the individual. The relational dynamics affects the collective mental health of the family.

ARE YOU PRESENT?

MK

So how do you think people can practice more active listening when they're communicating with their family members or colleagues?

Lynette

[laughing] That's very tough! Even as trained coaches, we have all these internal voices going through and we're so apt at just saying, eh just do this lah! But is that 'just do this' what the person actually needs? Are you listening to what the person is actually saying inside, or just on the surface? So how do you practice active listening? It's a good question.

Active listening is tough and requires conscious effort. It brings me back to the point where I said that during this pandemic, it was so easy for me to just run into back-to-back meetings online. But I realized that I was burning out and I was not present for the next meeting. I would be at my 100 per cent in my first meeting, and maybe 98 per cent in my next meeting, and etc. It spills over! And I realized I didn't give myself time to stop, think, recharge, before going into the next one. And that's detrimental to myself and the people around me, but more importantly, the people I am engaging with online.

So that's when I realized I needed to be present and that relates back to active listening. And I agree with you about being present because it's correlated. Active listening can only take place when you're fully present physically—mentally, psychologically, and physiologically. I constantly challenge myself: why are you there for the meeting? If you're there to have a meeting to engage with the person, to talk to the person, to get to know the person better, then be there. Don't be on your phone. Don't be doing something else. Be there 100 per cent to listen. And that's why good listeners are so difficult to find. But that's the first starting point. Only when you start listening—not hearing—will you be able to practice active listening. Because when you're actively listening, you're not only listening for what the person is saying, or verbalizing, but also what's actually going through inside them, and our body doesn't lie! You can see so much. It's like what psychology Professor Albert Mehrabian said, that the percentage of spoken is so miniscule at 7 per cent compared to the non-verbal cues made up of 55 per cent body language and 38 per cent voice and tone! And it's so true. Especially in the work that I do, even on Zoom or virtually, I can feel the difference in intonation or the words my clients say when I see their faces versus when I don't get to see their faces.

So active listening starts with listening 100 per cent and being present with the person, mentally, psychologically, and physiologically. Reduce the internal chatter that's going through you, that noise that's going through you, and just be 100 per cent present with them. That's where the connection is made, because that's where you start feeling and connecting with the person.

NO MAN IS AN ISLAND HIMSELF

MK

Nice. I want to ask you one last question. What does true connection mean to you? Let's look at true connection with the self, true connection with other people, and true connection with the community.

Lynette

So let's start with the self first, because I think that's where it all starts. I think that true connection with yourself is a discovery journey. I was like any other typical high-flyer working mum trying to manage both sides. Was I successful? I guess in the public eye

I was. I was in a well-paying job, good environment, great family, and kids were growing up well. But was I connected to myself? No. I struggled back then to be present to every conversation, especially when something was off balance, either at home if the kids were unwell, or at work if we were rushing for a deadline. That was the challenge.

I'm grateful that I had a lot of help and support from my family that allowed me to be very focused when I'm at work. But was I present with myself? No, not 100 per cent. I guess I'm comparing it with the lens that I have now. But if you asked that version of me five years or ten years ago whether I was present to myself, I would say yes, because I didn't have the level of awareness that I have now, and that's the difference. It comes back to what we talked about, awareness. Are you connected and aware of each emotion that's going through you? How do you connect with that emotion? And like the conversation I was having with my spouse the other day, how do you actually connect with that emotion and use it as a strength to bring about a greater impact to the work that you do? And that has helped me, I realize on hindsight, to stay focused when I'm at home and when I'm at work.
[short pause]

Lynette

As a coach, I think being connected means building trust and rapport with the client because when trust is not established, everything just becomes nonsense. [laughter] Nothing can cover up for the lack of trust. But when the client knows you will hold space for them, that's when rapport is built, that's where the trust is established, and that's when magic starts. The connection of trust is the foundation to the work I do.

But also, my heart aches for our youths. I've done mentoring work with Architects of Life, a social enterprise for youths at risk, and I volunteer with Limitless, a non-profit organization for youth-related causes. I think our youths today are privileged with the amount of resources that they have. But on the flip side, they have to deal with a fast-paced, constantly changing world, where what they learn may no longer be relevant when they graduate. How do we help them channel those resources correctly? And it's about maximizing what they have been given and moving them forward with what is inside them and what they are truly passionate about. I think that makes the difference, because you can see it in them, and when you reach them, when you're talking to them, you can see if it made sense to them or not. Otherwise they're IDK, I don't know, anything lor. [laughter] Their typical response which translates to don't talk to me anymore, you're not connecting to me.

MK

Yeah.

Lynette

So I train and facilitate programmes in schools and corporations. That is the way I stay connected to the community, to the work that I do, with the skills I've accumulated. It is my way of giving back. No man is an island, right? We are all here for a reason, so my purpose then is to give back and be that force for good, to create that positive impact on those around me. Even if it's just one person, it's okay! So be it. It doesn't stop me from doing what I see is the right thing to do

MK

Thank you. That was powerful.

CHAPTER SIX

Peace in Your Chaos

By Dr Jasmine Neo, Clinical Director and Head Consultant Psychologist, The Private Practice

In her therapy sessions, clients often grapple with the idea of taking care of themselves, as they find the act of doing so 'selfish'. Many people who suffer from depression or anxiety often find that they are their own greatest enemy, which causes them to have a difficult relationship with themselves. Jasmine shares that knowing yourself, having a relationship with yourself, having compassion with yourself, is key to having peace in the chaos.

MENTAL WELLNESS IS NOT AN 'I' THING, IT'S A 'WE' THING

MK

Why don't you share with me a little bit more about the work that you do?

Jasmine

The bulk of my training is in mental health. I was in KK[6] for about eight years. We helped women with their mood issues throughout their pregnancy. So before pregnancy, during pregnancy, after giving birth. So that's the part that's quite interesting, the maternal infant mental health that's also often neglected. But it's slowly gaining awareness now. So parenting attachment work, dealing with children, children's behavioural issues, anger issues. And it's quite interesting that this era of millennials is quite aware of their own mental health and the preservation of it. They don't only see therapy as, I have a problem then I come, but they actually want to build their self-awareness or build greater resilience. I see that shift in the clients that I do see, especially with the millennials.

MK

Got it, got it. And what are some of the mental stigmas that you've observed so far as a recurring pattern as you're working with these clients?

Jasmine

I think society has a part to play in whether it breeds mental illness. If you look at why a person is at risk of mental illness, it's always a combination of psychosocial factors, biological factors, family background, and their own experiences. And society has a big part to play in whether people seek help, feel ashamed of

---

[6] KK: KK Women's and Children's Hospital

seeking help, how fast they seek help, how people would look at them, or how being mentally ill might be viewed in society.

So in the clinic, there'll be times when there are more children in the room as compared to adults. It's quite jarring, and you wonder why. Why are so many children there? Why are they not well mentally? They're not supposed to have so many stresses, but here they are. And in my own clinic, I see a rise in anxiety and depression in children. And it's very sad. So if you ask me, it could be a combination of many systems. Education system, family system, expectations or just, how society is the chase, the not enough, the need to be successful in one way, a tabulated way. The need to prove themselves. And some people just can't fit into the system. Then where do they fit in? I know that the education system is evolving, but I don't know whether it's evolving fast enough. I think it's difficult to change on a systemic level and on a societal level.

There's this famous quote that has always stuck with me for a really long time since I got into mental health work. When 'I' is replaced with 'we', mental illness becomes mental wellness. That means mental wellness is not an 'I' thing, it's a 'we' thing. We all have a part to play.

SELF-LOVE ISN'T SELFISH

MK

One of the challenges that I personally face in this line is that I feel that everybody knows that collectively, we should play our parts together because one person's mental issues are going to create downward spirals, place stress and anxiety onto other people, and it also affects other people's mental health as a spillover. When we don't take care of ourselves enough, things like that happen, and one thing that is often underrated is self-love.

Jasmine

I agree. People always think that if I focus on myself, I'm selfish. But it's not selfish. It's actually the best way to take care of others. Because you're not being selfish when you take care of yourself—that's often the misconception—you're being self-focused. It's the same analogy as needing to wear your own oxygen mask first before you help others, right? If not, you are actually not helpful. So in a sense, taking care of yourself is the best way to take care of others, because if you don't take care of yourself, there's nothing really to give to others. That's something that keeps coming up in therapy too, the part about when I focus on myself, I'm selfish. And that has, it comes up in almost every session—

MK

[in disbelief] Every session?

Jasmine

Yeah, with individuals.

MK

[in more disbelief] Every session?

Jasmine

Yeah.

MK

So fundamentally, we're looking into a person's relationship with themselves? How healthy they are, how comfortable they are with themselves?

Jasmine

Yes. Actually, fundamentally, that is most important and that also is the root of a lot of depression and self-harm. Because you don't love yourself enough, you inflict harm onto yourself, right? It's the relationship you have with yourself. Because if you really love someone, how can you think of hurting them?

MK

[softly] Yeah. And sometimes, the way we understand love is very twisted. And it also contributes to the way we love ourselves, partly because we watched our families while we were growing up. Family traumas do play a large part in shaping our ideas of what love is and what love is not. We all learned from our parents as kids. They are our role models.

Jasmine

Yeah. I think it's quite complex, but relationships start with yourself.

MK

And how do you think people can build deeper relationships with themselves?

Jasmine

I think very simply, by treating themselves as a friend. For most people who suffer from depression or anxiety, they are their greatest enemy. They treat themselves as if they are their worst enemy. So I think it begins with thinking about how you would treat a friend and treating yourself the same way. If you were to speak to your friend the way you are speaking to yourself, would the person still be your friend?

MK

Yeah, so it begins with rewiring how we even build a relationship with ourselves. Can we accept ourselves for who we are and what we are? Do we even allow ourselves to go on a date with ourselves?

Jasmine

Yeah, do you even enjoy your own company? Do you even listen to yourself? Do you give yourself space, time, and give yourself what you require from others?

MK

And I guess the first step is for people to be self-aware that the way they are loving themselves is not exactly all they are capable of. And there are different layers of love. How can we love anybody if we don't love ourselves for who we are and what we are? Because it's going to be a reflection and manifestation of that. How we love other people shows our relationship with ourselves.

Jasmine

In a way, yes, but people would also argue that it's easier to love others than it is to love yourself, right?

[MK sighs heavily]

Jasmine

And they sometimes claim they don't know how to love or start loving themselves, but I think it starts with, how do you begin to love others? You treat them well, you're not judgemental, you're kind, compassionate, you build that friendship. Same thing applies to yourself; it's about building that friendship with yourself.

CREATING A LIFE THAT YOU DON'T NEED TO ESCAPE FROM

MK

One last question. How can people be at peace with themselves?

Jasmine

At peace?

MK

Correct. Now, this question has an underlying assumption that people are not at peace with themselves, therefore they want to look for inner peace. Therefore, they go into pilgrimages, meditation, yoga, to find that peace in themselves. But the context and understanding is, if a person needs to look into inner peace, it's because they're not at peace with themselves.
[short pause]

Jasmine

Wow, I think it's not an easy question to answer. I think it goes back to knowing yourself, the relationship you have with yourself, the amount of compassion you have for yourself, the permission you give yourself. It also starts with giving yourself that space and that time. People go to yoga retreats and meditation retreats because it gives them that space that time to dedicate to being with themselves. But after that retreat is over, there's some residual effects, but you'll need another retreat again.

MK

It's a vicious cycle. People think it's about doing programmes externally, but they need to recognize that it's their responsibility to do inner work. Nobody can clean their mess.

Jasmine

Yeah. I think it's the same as self-care. People think, oh, if I go for a massage or go shopping, if I carve this time out, it's self-care. But the ultimate definition of self-care is to create a life you don't need to escape from, and that's also listening to yourself and making some changes in your life, or doing what works for you, or living the life that is good for you, not what people tell you is good for you. I think that all contributes to peace and acceptance and calm. Stillness.

MK

A lot of people are looking for this stillness also because in our external environment, we don't get that. Things are moving too fast. It's too chaotic.

Jasmine

Not even externally. Internally, there's a lot of chaos, right?

MK

Correct. Because how we handle our external reality is also how we handle our internal reality. There's a very strong correlation. Got it. I like the quote I saw as I was walking up the stairs—

Jasmine

Peace in your chaos?

MK

Yeah! You came up with it?

Jasmine

Yeah!

MK

Amazing.

CHAPTER SEVEN

What Happens When Trauma Happens in Your Own Backyard

By Andrea Chan, Senior Assistant Director at NCSS, Assistant Director of TOUCH Mental Wellness, TOUCH Integrated Family Group

Having travelled to a number of South Asian countries in her teens, Andrea was moved by the traumatic situations children in those countries had to deal with, such as the death of a parent, or abuse. While she initially planned to work overseas, she eventually chose to stay in Singapore when she saw the cases of trauma at home.

THE ISSUE WITH SELF-DIAGNOSING

MK

Why don't you share with me about the work that you do?

Andrea

We work according to three pillars on mental health for youths—education, intervention, and advocacy. Take education for example—we want to use very innovative technology to teach youths because we need to capture their interest and on top of that we want to have high retention rates. Then intervention—what are the latest therapies and modalities that are out there that have been researched on, that work best in different conditions? It's something that we constantly look out and read a lot of journals for. And the last one is advocacy. I'm sure my colleague Joel will tell you that we go on Instagram, we go on TikTok, we post pictures, and on top of that in the past before COVID, there were a lot of roadshows. I especially liked the roadshows because I got to have conversations with different people.

MK

What are some of the mental health stigmas you've observed while doing all this work you do?

Andrea

Because I deal predominantly with children and youth, parents are a big crucial factor. That is why I tell my team all the time to target advocacy efforts on youths, because they are the next generation of parents. It's too much to teach an old dog new tricks, so why don't we set the conditions right for the next generation? I think one of the biggest struggles is when parents reject intervention because they say I don't want my child to have that record in their employment. I don't want it to be in the medical records, it affects insurance. Or I don't want my child to be on medication for the rest of their lives. That's something I hear quite a fair bit, not so much from the youths themselves. In fact, I have a lot of youths who are very open, and if anything, my youths are too open. They come in and tell me Andrea, I think I have depression or Andrea, I think I have this and that. Then I say, what makes you think you have that? The common reply is I went to Google my symptoms and this is what Google says. So Google becomes their psychiatrist and I think oftentimes, they might be too quick to judge themselves or too quick to tick off the list and it becomes a learnt behaviour. I think I have anxiety, and anxiety displays such symptoms, so I start to subconsciously act this way. That is the issue with youths.

MK

Alright. Tell me more details about what causes these behavioural patterns. What are the consequences of self-diagnosing?

Andrea

When you self-diagnose, it's very scary because you have a perception or preconceived idea of what your identity is. So they kind of link their perceived mental health condition with their identity and that makes recovery very difficult. For example, let's say, depression. Depression is so common, and we teach depression signs and symptoms so often. So with depression, what they do is, they Google and they see that one of the signs of depression is a sense of hopelessness. And in all teenagers' lives, because of their fluctuating hormones, because of puberty, there'll be times when they feel a sense of hopelessness, a sense of helplessness. There'll be times when they feel down, but this doesn't mean they have depression. But if they self-diagnose that they have depression, then they allow themselves to stay in their condition and not get out of it. In fact, subconsciously, they encourage such behaviours because it puts a label on them and gives them a reason to stay that way. But it may not be true. So that's a major danger when it comes to self-diagnosing. In TOUCH, we do not diagnose. We work with symptoms. Hence, I'm very cautious when a client or youth comes in and says I believe I have this condition because I checked it online. So generally, I tend to be more cautious and have more than one source of reporting. Like hearing from parents, best friend, siblings, and teachers, if they allow. That will give me a more holistic picture.

MENTAL HEALTH REPRESENTATION IN THE MEDIA

MK

Tell me more about other stigmas around mental health.

Andrea

I think there is one very common stigma, which is the misconception that anyone with mental health conditions is violent, so I must stay clear of them. I think we have made progress since the beginning of this year, but generally when you read newspapers and they say that this person abused the maid or abused the helper, one of the sweeping statements is she is diagnosed with something, adjustment disorder, depression, things like that, but there is no write-up on what that condition is. There is also no link to what the condition has to do with the case. So just because you have a mental health condition doesn't mean you're driven to act that way, because there are people with mental health conditions that don't abuse their helpers. They don't murder their children, for that matter. So when we make sweeping statements like that in the newspaper and they say that so and so pleads insanity or whatever condition, and the psychiatrist certifies that they have this condition, it becomes very confusing to the public because subconsciously, people link that violent act to that mental health condition. It's not helpful. Which is why one of the recommendations I made was that if you want to talk about the mental health condition, you should talk about how it has contributed to the case. But increasingly I think responsible reporters do write that the judge says it has no effect, did not impair his judgement when he did the act, things like that.

I think one of the biggest red flags that got me noticing this was when the news came about the boy who murdered his mother and his grandma. In the media it says that he went for a psychiatric assessment but after that, there have been no news until now. So it's really up to you to assume that the fact that you went for a psychiatric assessment means you might have a mental health condition. Then people will assume you definitely have a condition because no normal person will go and kill their mother and grandmother, right? Then automatically we send the subtle message that mental health conditions are violent.

STIGMA ENLARGES THE INDIVIDUAL DISCONNECT

Andrea

The other stigma that I feel is very common stems from helplessness rather than despising or rejecting people with mental health conditions. I do have a lot of people on the ground reporting that they try not to talk to people with mental health conditions because they don't know how to help. So there's this general avoidance because they feel or think that people with mental health conditions take up a lot of time and energy, and that you need to have a special skill set in order to know how to help. And because I can't, then I stay away. But what I always say is that when you isolate them, it makes recovery very very difficult, because it's a very long journey and it's very hard to walk alone. And when you isolate them, all the more they don't get to practice survival skills that are important for them, so it's harder for them to integrate into society.

MK

So the disconnect inside them is actually enhanced even more, and it makes the recovery much harder, much more complicated as well?

Andrea

Correct. So for example, in our approach in mental health intervention, something we do all the time is we ensure that there's a strong support system surrounding this individual. So in some sense, it's similar to what they say: it takes a village to raise a child. It takes a community to help a person recover. When that community is missing, it's a very difficult journey to walk on their own because they don't have people to sound off. Talking to people could be one effective coping strategy for them, but now they don't have that at all. All the isolation could again be a trigger because then when they go out in public, there's this fear. They don't dare to meet people again. It becomes a trigger. So I don't go out, I isolate myself at home, then I don't leave the house. It becomes a perpetual cycle that they are caught in.

IT'S TIME WE LOOK INTO MENTAL WELLNESS

MK

Well, I'm just thinking, if we already know these things are happening, how come intervention is still so difficult? How come even though all these things sound very common sense to us, it's not commonly practiced?

Andrea

Something that I always say is that the one good thing that came out of COVID is increased mental health advocacy and awareness. Because when you're stuck at home or living in this environment that is constantly changing, everyone experiences some signs or symptoms of stress, be it the frustration we feel, the sense of helplessness, lack of control, or insecurity. So I think it has increased empathy in most people. And it is always a challenge to instil a sense of empathy in people! It's difficult to help people understand that sometimes when you're talking to someone with depression, it's not as easy as saying why don't you just snap out of it, what's the big deal? Because of the lack of empathy, people may not know that some of these behaviours are very hard to control and manage.

So how do you teach empathy if the only way to do it is to put yourself in another person's shoes? You can only do so if you are able to create an environment where you can put yourself in that person's shoes. And again, there are many different types of mental health conditions. There is schizophrenia, there are personality disorders, eating disorders, depression, anxiety etc. How do we then create an environment that increases empathy for all conditions?

MK

A conscious environment, how do we create that?

Andrea

Yes, that is the difficult part, I feel, in making that change.

And in a very pragmatic society, in a society that thinks very rationally, how do you link the heart to the brain? Again the statements that I made just now, like stop being so dramatic, what are the chances of that happening (probability of catastrophe)? Those are very rational thoughts. If I'm a rational being, I can come up with those thoughts, like yeah, what are the chances of that happening? I should calm down. But people with a mental health condition are not in that rational state. So then how can I help that mentally-well individual link that knowledge to the heart so that they know what the other person is feeling? It's the difficult part, I feel.

MK

I was thinking about what you said earlier on. For the most part we're not taught to understand our emotions. We go to school but we don't learn these things.

Andrea

It's the culture of Singapore, right? I mean look at the core values of Singapore, no one owes you a living. That's a very rational one, you're supposed to work hard. It's a Singaporean culture. Is that wrong? I don't think so, because of how nation-building works and how we needed to survive with no resources. I think it's a practical and the fastest approach to bringing a nation up. But now that we have progressed to a more stable state, how can we move beyond that and focus on other aspects which were previously neglected?

MK

How can we inculcate more emotional and mental wellness? More self-awareness?

Andrea

Correct. And with a youth group, or even an adult group, with a population that is so educated to have accessibility to almost everything in the world, how can we look beyond just economics, beyond practicality, beyond logic, to talk a little more about the heart, the softer aspect of things? Can we afford to talk about them now? I think yes. Are we going to undo what happened previously? I think there needs to be a certain change, but I think it doesn't mean we have to totally undo the values we have learnt all these years. I think those are still useful and those are still foundational, but let's build on this foundation.

TRAUMA SHOULDN'T ROB YOU OF A FAIR CHANCE IN LIFE

MK

Actually, I'm very curious. How did you get into this particular line of work?

Andrea

I think it's a very good question! I would have to say that my personal speciality is in trauma. It started very young. When I was seventeen and finished year one in JC, I started travelling quite a bit in South Asian countries. I've been to India, Nepal, Pakistan, Sri Lanka, all these places and I stayed there for a couple of months at one go. I've worked with women who are abused, and worked in orphanages where children witness the death of their parents, and I witnessed the ongoing abuse they experience in a children's home. It was easier for me to cope then because it was harm done outside of my own comfort zone, right? Singapore is so safe, Singapore is so secure, so I wanted to give that help outside. But as I did my studies, I realized that I wanted to do more, so I went into this line. I think when I started seeing cases, it was like do I go overseas or stay in Singapore? But I thought Singapore would be a good starting point for someone very new like me to learn these skills before I go to these developing countries. I mean if you go to India and you say you're a counselling psychologist, nobody knows what you're talking about or who you are. So I wanted to build my skills in Singapore first. But because I started my career in Singapore, it opened my eyes to see harm done in my own backyard, and that affected me a lot. Because it's easy to leave a country and come back home and say home sweet home, I'm safe. But then it's very hard to come back home and see that my home is not safe, there are people hurting, my neighbour is hurting, a fellow Singaporean is hurting, a child in my vicinity is hurting, and I think that was very difficult for me, especially for children and youth.

Why I go into trauma is because trauma is so complex. Trauma is so life-changing and damaging, especially as a child. How do I give the child equity, you know? Giving the child better chances. That's where my heart is. I think growing up there is this sense of fairness and justice that now as an adult I think is very hard to realize. At the back of my head, there is always that I want that child to have a fair chance, because something so unfortunate happened shouldn't rob the child of that fair chance. So I wanted to do my bit to ensure that the child has that fair chance at life.

MK

Got it. So your specialization is in trauma work, dealing with childhood traumas?

Andrea

Yes, my favourite is also trauma work. I think that there is very high adrenaline because every day is new, every day is different. One of my mentors during the early years of my career, one of my first bosses, said that your client needs your hand-holding to walk through the darkest parts of their life and I think for me, personally, it's also that challenge and the realization that it is a privilege for the client to say that I want to hold your hand to walk through the darkest parts of my life. And they want to see how I react. Will I reject them because I see that darkness in their lives? Will I cringe at the darkness in their lives? And that's something that stayed with me because I want to make sure that in that darkness, I can be that light, I can show them some of that love, some of that care, even in that darkness hopefully they can find some hope.

BE BRAVE TO TELL YOUR STORY

MK

Meaningful. Very powerful. The final question I have for you would be, if you had a message you would like to say to the world, to the public around mental health, suicide prevention, what would that be?

Andrea

I think there would be two messages to give two different kinds of people.

To the general public, this is something I always say: that mental health conditions are very much like fever, flu. We can manage symptoms and we can still live a very normal life. So when you have a fever, when you have a flu, you go and see a doctor without thinking twice. So in the same way, when you have a mental health condition, why not seek help ASAP, because the faster you seek help, the more effective and less intensive therapy needs to be. So that's one.

To the other group, those who are already experiencing signs and symptoms, I just want to say you're not alone and your bravery to tell your story and stand up there and share how you've had successes, how you've had bad days, really helps people standing on the outside empathize or see for themselves that people with mental health conditions can indeed live normal lives. People with mental health conditions can have bad days just like anyone else can have bad days. What can we do when you have those bad days, or how can we celebrate with you when you have those good days? You be our teacher. Because there's no one who can teach more powerfully than the ones who experience it themselves. So be brave and tell your story. We are rallying around you and with you in this.

CHAPTER EIGHT

Trauma and the Collective Suffering

By Buvenasvari Pragasam,
Registered Art Psychotherapist,
Founder of Solace Art Psychotherapy

We all experience challenges in our childhood that shape who we are, and our perception of the world is shaped and reinforced by these experiences over time. If we do not work on our own healing, we continuously inflict harm and suffering on the people around us, thus the collective suffering from our past traumas. Buvi talks about how trauma is manifested, and how societal stigmas create multiple barriers preventing people from seeking help.

ART THERAPY WAS LIFE CHANGING

MK

I'm interested in your journey as an art therapist in trauma-informed works. What made you decide to enter the mental health profession?

Buvi

It was quite an interesting journey and none of it was planned. I started off as an investigation officer and decided that I wanted to move into the field of psychology. It was exactly ten years ago when I completed my BA in Psychology and became an educational therapist. As an educational therapist, I was involved in providing intervention programmes for students in the mainstream schools who were diagnosed with dyslexia or other kinds of learning differences. Previously it was known as dyslexia and now it's called specific learning differences in the DSM-5.

MK

I used to have mild dyslexia.

Buvi

I have mild to moderate dyslexia as well, and I didn't know until the later part of my journey.

MK

Well, I didn't know until I was eighteen.

Buvi

I didn't know until I was working as an educational therapist. I only knew about it when I learnt about the symptoms during my training as an educational therapist. What I experienced and the symptoms of dyslexia matched. Furthermore, doing a few online assessments confirmed that I might be having mild to moderate dyslexia. Having that revelation helped me a lot in understanding the difficulties I underwent during my schooling days and it was liberating.

Though I really enjoyed my work as an educational therapist, my dad fell ill towards the end of those years. So I had to quit my job just to stay with my dad through the last few months and I eventually lost him. I went through a grieving process of six to eight months. I couldn't function, I couldn't go to work, I couldn't do anything. During that period, my cousin asked me if I would be interested in becoming an art therapist since I enjoy art and have completed BA Psychology. That led me to pursue my Master's in Art Therapy.

I embarked on the art therapy journey not knowing what it would entail. I thought, *how* difficult could it be? Little did I know that it would be a rigorous, life-transforming journey. During the course of studies, we had to clock over 800 hours of clinical internships. I chose to work with female adolescents with complex trauma. That was one of the best and most eye-opening experience for me. I realized a lot about art therapy through my own personal therapy journey and my clients' journeys. I learnt how art therapy can help to express and transform. The transformation was evident and visible with my clients. That gave me a lot of confidence and assurance that this is the path that I'm going to embark on to help people process their past trauma through art therapy.

So I began to evaluate and keep track of the effectiveness of my art therapy sessions. I needed to show people that art therapy can improve people's lives. Some people think that a lot of things can't be changed, but no, there are a lot of things that you can change if you just allow yourself and your body to process. And I started to get intrigued by how our body protects us, of course not exactly in healthy ways. So these experiences and my personal therapy journey brought me to trauma-informed art therapy practice. When I saw my personal transformation, I started to understand people around me better, and I also noticed transformations in my clients, and that reassured me further. So I started my private practice, Solace Art Psychotherapy, providing trauma-informed art therapy to youths and adults.

MK

Tell me about the mental health stigma you've faced in Singapore. Because you deal with different groups of people, you'll be able to see common threads when it comes to mental health stigmas in Singapore. Tell me one thing.

Buvi

One thing? There are many things!

MK

Then tell me those many things.

TROUBLE WITH TAKING THE FIRST STEP

Buvi

I will share different reasons why certain stigmas exist. Firstly, there is a 'us-versus-them' mentality instead of an understanding that we all are on a spectrum of mental health. Many may be happy to advocate or support mental health movements, but they may not take the first step to assess their mental health and seek support if necessary.

Secondly, it is seen that seeking mental health support means you have a mental disorder, are mentally unstable or that something is wrong with you. One does not need to be diagnosed with a mental disorder in order for them to seek support from a mental health professional. Feeling stressed or overwhelmed can be a reason to seek support from a mental health professional.

Thirdly, some may have the 'I am managing' mentality. It is difficult to have a clear indication as to when to draw the line. Constantly having disrupted sleep, loss of appetite and interest, tiredness, may seem normal and common. But these could also be symptoms of not managing your mental health well. Rather than seeking support from a mental health professional, people may continue to go about with their day-to-day activities as they may seem 'normal'.

Some are afraid that they might be labelled as mentally unfit and therefore worried that their career might be affected due to the stigma against poor mental health. They are worried that friends and family will view them differently if anyone finds out that they are seeking therapy. I have ever heard a family forcefully stopping one of their family members from seeking professional help to process the trauma. We have a long way to go in Singapore to normalizing seeing a mental health professional and talking about their healing journey openly to friends and family.

All these are some of the stigma against mental health that stops people from stepping forward to seek support from a mental health professional. For art therapy specifically, people think it's for children or elderly. I have people who come to me and say I do art therapy for myself and I'm like, even I can't do art therapy for myself.

MK

You can't do that. You get trapped in a psychological loop.

Buvi

Sometimes I'll just ask oh how do you do that, and they'll say oh I do colouring, I engage in some art-making, and that's really good because it is therapeutic in nature, it is art as therapy. Everyone can do that.

MK

But it's not art therapy.

Buvi

Yeah it's not really addressing the issue but it is giving you the comfort and the release that you need. But it's temporary.

The misconception is that art therapy is a fun activity, it's for children, and it's relaxing, therefore I can do it myself because it's so available. People think that by drawing and colouring they are helping their mental wellbeing. Yes it does, but my question is, to what extent?

LISTENING TO WHAT'S UNSAID

MK

Is there a stigma you encountered that left a deep impact on you?

Buvi

I attended a talk on suicide. The sharing was impactful but I realized they were all talking about one thing people who have attempted suicide and have either survived or openly shared about their suicidal ideation.

People might think that those who self-harm are displaying signs of crying for help and seeking attention. To me, it's a huge sign saying that they're crying for help without crying for help. But what often happens too is that a lot of people who are suicidal don't show or take steps that leave scars. For example, popping pills may not leave scars or signs that people can notice. So when somebody attempts suicide and succeeds, they will say that I was just speaking to him and he was fine, I don't know why he committed suicide, he didn't show signs, because everyone talks about the typical image of someone who is suicidal, but not everyone who is suicidal will fit into that profile.

What people fail to see is those who are suffering in silence. People often talk about those who are louder than those who are silent. So the silent ones are missed out, even in schools. When a teacher points out someone who has behavioural problems, it's often those who are acting out, who openly show that they are struggling, screaming, getting angry, etc. But what about those who are fighting in silence? It's not in their personality to scream, shout, and walk out. They may submit their homework on time, they may come to class, they may have friends, but they may also be suicidal or depressed, but nobody notices that, so those are the ones I'm most worried about. Of course, we are now talking about such issues, so it's still a great step forward, but I also wish that people will look at those who suffer in silence.

There's this widespread perception that when you're mentally unwell, it's visible. No, it's not. Even for myself, I have suicidal tendencies whenever I'm facing with emotionally overwhelming scenarios. And if I were to end my life one day, people would be left wondering why such a bubbly, strong person, would end her life. But no one would realize that I have my own struggles that are unseen.

And also, when it is visible, people don't know how to provide support, and may encourage one to distract themselves and try to make themselves 'happier' instead of seeking professional support to address the core issues causing them to be unwell. Stigma is a huge topic.

MK

What do you think is really holding them or stopping them from expressing their truth? I don't know whether it makes sense or not.

Buvi

I think it makes sense.

MK

What do you think is causing this situation where people are talking about it but not looking into it because they're suffering in silence? Also, what is making these people silent?

Buvi

This is just my personal opinion. I've thought about this many times, but I think it is about having awareness. They might not even be aware that what they're going through is affecting them. That's the biggest one. I've seen it in my friends too. Even in myself. When I was experiencing burnout, I didn't know that it was burnout. I thought it was something else. Because I'm in this field of mental wellness, I was more interested in finding out. So I took steps, I visited my own therapist and engaged in self-care activities. Then I realized oh my god this is burnout. So to have that awareness in the first place was crucial. But to have awareness, you need to have knowledge. So more people need to talk, more people need to share, it needs to be normalized, we need to be educated. Through sharing our personal experiences, more people might be able to relate and gain insights and awareness about what they might be experiencing. There are people within my circle who are opening up about their therapy journey to help others in the process. But somehow seeing a mental health professional is not in our culture or practice.

Just like when you have an injury, you must do certain things to treat the wound. Psychological first aid should be taught to everyone too. Once they have the awareness and the knowledge then maybe they might speak to someone whom they trust, and then maybe they might take the next step. So there are many layers that need to be in place before they come to the step of getting help. And it cannot be a one-man effort. It has to be a community effort.

For example, I'm sharing that I have suicidal tendencies that people may not know of. Because I am hoping that when I share, someone else might share too. I also experienced burnout. The burnout was a result of the pandemic issue last year. I didn't realize how much I was working last year. I shared that realization with people despite it being quite *paiseh*[7] for me especially since I am in the mental health sector. But I'm happy to share because

---

[7] Paiseh: Singapore slang for embarrassing

I want to take the first step to share with people so they might recognize that they are experiencing burnout. And therapists, counsellors, psychologists, psychiatrists are human too and they too need to seek professional help. I wonder how many mental health professionals actually attend their own personal therapy sessions.

Another event that impacted me was when I did an advocacy talk with a hospital. We created a stress-o-metre. So there were stickers to indicate your stress levels. Green stickers meant no stress, yellow meant getting there but managing, red meant quite *jialat*.[8] Everyone, when casually asked, would say that they were super stressed, highly stressed, a lot of things to manage! But when I got them to choose a sticker and indicate on the stress-o-metre, most people chose yellow stickers. They would tell me that oh I'm managing, because they're so afraid that I was going to sell them something to encourage them to go and get help. Either way, I was going to encourage them to get help, whether they're stressed or not. They were so worried about choosing red stickers despite being highly stressed. The yellow sticker was the most popular choice. Few people chose green; even fewer people chose red.

The stigma is real and affects people in many ways. Stress, burnouts, emotional problems, past problems. Trauma is a big word, it's not easy to say that I have experienced trauma.

WHAT DO YOU WANT TO DO ABOUT IT?

MK

The word trauma has a lot of negative stigmas around it. The first thing we've got to do is realize that trauma is a neutral force. Your greatest gifts also come from your deepest wounds. Trauma is just a force that hits you and creates a dent.

---

[8] Jialat: Singapore slang for a dire situation

Buvi

Now that we are talking about trauma and psyche, there are different angles and perspectives to it. From the neurological perspective, the right brain blocks out certain traumatic memories. Trauma is stored in our bodies and in the right brain, but how do we access them if our right brain blocks them out? In the book *The Body Keeps the Score*, the psychiatrist Dr. Bessel van der Kolk shares that trauma is stored in the right brain, which blocks out memories in order for you to function as per usual. So sometimes people assume that their childhood was great and they move along with life until something 'hits' them and the body responds. The right brain is not able to give the visual or memories as to why you're responding in a certain way and sometimes you just respond not knowing where it's coming from.

So this is where art therapy comes in. Art accesses the right brain as it's a right-brain activity. When you attend art therapy sessions, it might gently assess those memories in a non-intrusive manner and it could flow out through the artwork. When both the body and the mind are involved in the creation of the artwork, that's when it connects, and issues or trauma surfaces up through the artwork. These are issues that my clients didn't even indicate that they've experienced before, and then trauma after trauma comes out in the following sessions.

MK

Well, trauma happens to everybody, it's just that we're unaware of it. We don't even know how we became the person we are today. We think that we know who we are but we don't realize that we're not fixed in one personality. It's because of the multiple traumas, the force that split us that creates different personalities and inner voices. Some voices tell you that you're not good enough, some voices tell you that you're not worthy enough. You spend your life chasing after the things that don't really matter to you because it comes from your history. Then the question is, what have you been living for?

Buvi

Agreed. So it kind of adds a layer to an actual healthy adult. Every layer, every experience, every person they meet keeps adding layer after layer.

MK

And sometimes because of certain traumas you've experienced, you told yourself that you know what, I'm not going to let my kid experience what I experienced when I was young. And you spend your whole life trying to teach your kid to deviate from the path that you had so that they won't have to experience what you did. But in reality that's not what they need. It's the same saying that we can only accept the love we deserve and the love that we receive is not what we need.

Buvi

Sometimes parents overcompensating for what they didn't have is also not a good thing. Because they're trying to fulfil that need to protect their child but actually they're not exactly protecting their child.

MK

They're just protecting themselves, the nine-year-old them who hasn't broken free from their own trauma, and they are just projecting onto their child when they don't recognize that their child is a different person from them.

Buvi

This can have a huge impact on them and not just their loved ones but their bosses, their colleagues, whoever they work or interact with. And you can't avoid interacting with others because you are part of society, so you end up co-suffering. Because people who are struggling with their past trauma respond in a particular way to the people around them, and the people around them have to bear the pain as well. It is collective. Hence, I'm doing my best to advocate about trauma.

It is possible to process and address past difficult experiences.

HAPPINESS IS JUST AN EMOTION

MK

Let's talk about that. How do you think we can address stigmas so that we can improve the quality of mental health in Singapore?

Buvi

How do we address that? Wow. I think we are already taking baby steps and I have to appreciate what has been done so far. But it is something that we cannot expect to change fast. In fact, COVID really helped to expedite certain things because a lot of people were turning inwards during lockdown and reflecting on themselves. I think that helped unlock a lot of doubts and questions about mental health and we have to continue advocating.

However, during COVID a lot of people started to advocate for mental health without adequate knowledge and I felt that was frustrating because we are already dealing with one level of 'tsunami', now there's a different kind of problem coming out. For example, everything became 'self-care'. Indulgence and self-care, there's a huge difference. It's like taking sugar to perk yourself up versus taking a proper meal to give you full energy.

MK

And these days you know, every time you talk about self-love, people will associate that with being selfish. It seems that everything you do with yourself, there's always a negative association.

Buvi

There's always something else you need to counter. So when the pandemic happened and people were turning inwards, there was also another set of problems arising where everybody wanted to be part of this trend, like because everyone's talking about mental health, I also want to talk about mental health and self-care. Self-care is not a fun activity.

MK

It doesn't work that way. You know, I have a lot of critiques on this issue. Everyone was talking about mental health during the pandemic but mental health has always been an issue that's been around, not just during the pandemic. COVID merely triggered some issues so you end up looking at the same issues that have always been there.

Buvi

It was just amplified during that time.

MK

Exactly. And you know, most of the time, we look outwards for answers. But once COVID and lockdown happened, we're shut off and we're forced to look inwards. But without an internal map, how do we look inside ourselves? Our whole life, nobody ever taught us or trained us to look inwards. We don't even understand that emotions have layers.

Buvi

Yes, and I dislike it when people say there are bad emotions and good emotions. Emotions are just emotions, period.

MK

But the more you try to suppress it, the more it's going to burst out. Whatever you don't deal with will always come back.

Buvi

Correct. So whenever people say oh I'm feeling sad, how can I not feel sad? Or how can I control my emotions? First of all, you don't control your emotions, you don't need to control emotions. Emotions give you information, it's what you're feeling, period. Experience it, ask yourself where it's coming from, that's it. And then work on it, as opposed to I shouldn't be feeling sad, I shouldn't be feeling jealous. I mean you can feel jealous, who said it's bad?

MK

I mean if controlling our emotions really works, how come there's so many people having issues? How come millionaires and billionaires have the same issue, the same emptiness even after they hit the peak of success?

Buvi

Yes, because it's not been addressed.

MK

And some people think that money can solve all problems, just because you have a little bit more money.

Buvi

Because your cognitive or logical brain tries to give you answers that you think you can look for. But if you don't address the root cause, no matter what you look for on the outside, it doesn't solve the problem on the inside.

MK

Exactly. You're still going to look for compensation. We come into this world with nothing, we're going to leave this world with nothing. In the end, when you die, you can't really say that you lived a rich life because money is not what makes life rich. Money is only an access point to get into certain experiences. It's a ticket, but it's not everything.

Buvi

Then my question is, what made you reach that point? So again, it goes back down to why there is the need to look for that.

MK

Why is there the need to chase, why is there the need to prove that money will make you successful? On one hand we need to look into our individual traumas. On the other hand we need to look into the collective societal trauma. We have been taught a certain belief system that we need to have money to buy freedom. It is a very human condition to look for freedom.

Buvi

But everything has its good and bad.

MK

Correct, and the problem is too many people are unaware of that. Because they are barely handling their own functionality, so need to begin looking into this thing called functional consciousness. How conscious are we?

Buvi

It's a very good question. I think we are very far from being very conscious. Compared to five years ago, I think we are in a better place where more people are being conscious, being mindful, being aware, but to what extent? I'm not sure.

So that's why more people should really come forward to share their stories and really normalize things. Understand, create that consciousness, that awareness and apply it. Because some people just listen and stop there. It's the application part where they struggle.

MK

It's a habit thing. You deal with your trauma, you deal with the emotional baggage, you still need the habits to correct the way of living because your body is used to performing in a certain way, so it naturally defaults back into that state.

Buvi

It's easy to go into that state. It's a comfort zone.

MK

That's why manifestation is important. Because that's the most tangible reality and proof that our life has changed.

Buvi

And this is an ongoing battle. More people should come forward, to be aware of what the root cause of their issues are and to address it. That's what we all need to do. I'm glad that the government is doing more for mental health and that people are coming forward to say that mental health is not just the professional's job, but it's everybody's job. Everybody needs to understand this and apply it. We are often taught to think but we were not allowed or taught or encouraged to feel.

MK

We've been trained all our lives in school how to think, but no one ever taught us how to feel. We don't understand our emotions. We live our lives thinking that we can't feel happiness, anger, and sadness all at the same time. We think that they are all independent from one another, but emotions also have layers within themselves and emotions can happen with one another.

Buvi

Yup, that will take a toll on our bodies as psychosomatic symptoms.

MK

We don't even understand how our body and our systems operate. Which begs the question—we spend our whole lives chasing after these paper degrees. Six years in primary school, four to five years in secondary school, two to three years in junior college, and then in university you spend about another four to five years. Let's say you want to go for a Master's and PhD, which takes about six years in total. So in total, we spend twenty-two years of our lives chasing after that paper to say that we're an expert in that particular thing. But did we spend twenty-two years of our lives working on who we are as a person? Trying to figure ourselves out? Our potential? What we were meant to do? My answer is, we didn't. We can barely afford forty-eight hours looking into ourselves.

Buvi

Let's not even talk about forty-eight. Let's talk about just an hour.

MK

We can't even sit still. Ask you to do meditation, you can't because too many disturbances already.

Buvi

Let's not even talk about meditation, but just to sit down and do nothing.

MK

Be with yourself.

Buvi

Yeah. Just look out the window.

MK

All the restlessness, all the anxiety, all the impatience, all the stuff that you haven't dealt with—all will show up.

I always hear the same stories, and it doesn't matter what kind of social titles you carry. It's the same issue. You can be the CEO of a company, you can be the manager of a corporation running a nine to five job, you can be a housewife, you can be a student as well—everybody has something they're struggling with.

Buvi

Just to highlight it's very important to ask for the credentials, experiences, and the area of expertise of the mental health professional. It is good to have attended one to two sessions before deciding whether to continue working with them. Because what you're working on is yourself, your work, your life, so you would want to ensure that whoever you're sharing with, your therapist, your doctor, your clinician, whoever you're talking to knows their stuff because you're entrusting your life and sharing your deeper stuff. So this is something I've been advocating as well, because there are a lot of people who take the first step of seeking help, but it doesn't work well because of poor therapist-client fit or poor therapy-client fit, and they easily give up on seeking help entirely because it didn't work. You have to continuously look for someone until it fits well.

MK

I want to thank you for the work that you do. I think that it's amazing. More people need to know about the work that you do.

Buvi

I'm very thankful that my clients who have 'graduated' from our therapy sessions have not come back again which is a great sign. Whenever I do a check-in with them just to ensure that everything's okay, most of the time it's been positive and I'm glad. Positive doesn't mean fantastic. It could mean that the week went horrible but they've been managing well. That is positive to me. Not like no problems at all. I would be worried if that was the case. Really? No problems? Means something's not right. Cannot be no problems. It's about how you face problems. And how you deal with them. So I'm glad so far that it has been working great. I'm hoping to grow Solace in a way that I can continue amplifying the support that we can give to people by accessing the right brain, accessing the body, by accessing the unconscious in a non-intrusive and non-intimidating manner.

I'm not very good with language. I'm dyslexic, so I usually struggle with helping by talking. But with artmaking, it does all the work in terms of addressing the trauma, revealing the problem, and also healing, and I'm just facilitating the process. And everything flows from the client and flows back to the client so I'm just here to hold the space and to facilitate the session.

MK

Thank you. The role of a healer is not to heal but to facilitate the space for healing to begin.

Buvi

Yes, and to empower them. That's our tagline. Empowering you through art. We facilitate and hold the space safe enough for you to have your healing. What you went through is for you to process. I can never fully empathize because I didn't go through it entirely, but I can feel to a certain extent. But at the end of the day, you got to feel, you got to acknowledge, you got to process.

CHAPTER NINE

It's Not Their Fault for Having a Mental Health Condition

By Ying Jia, Frontline Worker

As a frontline worker, Ying Jia supports the planning of services both in the hospital and the community. She shares that mental health is a multi-layered issue, and we are currently lacking a holistic approach and perspective to resolving the issue, especially among lower-income groups. Asian families also have the tendency to carry the narrative that it is our fault for not taking care of ourselves and having a mental health condition, preventing people from speaking up and seeking help as they feel ashamed of their condition. She hopes that people will respond with empathy and create an open environment for conversations to flourish.

A HOLISTIC PERSPECTIVE ON MENTAL HEALTH

MK

Could you share with us what you do in your work?

Ying Jia

I support the planning of services both in the hospital as well as in the community. The work I do includes the portfolio of mental health and caring for people in the lower-income groups. What we try to do is really go upstream and prevent mental health conditions even before they begin. Intervening early as well as building resilience in the community.

MK

As part of the planning team, when you plan for services and care for the people on the ground, what are some of the challenges that you face?

Ying Jia

Okay, so talking about challenges first. I think it's probably something that happens across Singapore or other countries as well, and it's that a lot of things happen from the top-down. So it's the leaders from the top who might not be very in touch with what's actually happening on the ground. They often think oh this population group needs this thing, so let's roll this out without finding out if this is really what people on the ground need and want. This is one of the main challenges and something that's frustrating for me personally because I'm just at the lowest level, which is just execution, so I might not have a say in whether these things really need to be done or not. We just do it and when we evaluate these services, we find that it's not as effective or helpful to the people as we'd like it to be. So we need a mindset shift to interact with people on the ground to find out what they actually need. So that's what we, my department at least, are trying to do. We are engaging the population groups that we serve. For example, if we're working with the lower-income groups, we will actually speak with them perhaps through focus groups or interviews to find out what it is that they're facing, their challenges, and the gaps in the current system.

Other challenges are that because mental health is multifaceted. There are just too many things that need to be addressed beyond the individual. And so far, we have been focusing too much on the individual without looking beyond that.

MK

I'm hearing that there's a lot of disengagement between the people who are planning and the people who are on the ground. What do you think causes this divide, and what are some of the impacts that you see?

Ying Jia

Let's just take this example: we are trying to simultaneously improve both the physical and mental health of the lower-income groups that we're serving. What we're realizing currently is that a lot of it is focused on just meeting their basic financial needs. So they might seek help from social services and only receive short-term financial assistance, for example, but that doesn't actually solve the root cause. It just traps them in the poverty cycle, facing all the domestic violence and family issues that are not addressed. It's challenging because our solutions are very focused on the surface problems, which are the basic needs, without directly addressing the fundamental issues. What we need is greater societal support and better understanding of their vulnerabilities. There's this divide where people on top think that they just need the finances and they can get out of it and solve all their other problems, but on the ground, while their finances might be their immediate problem, they also have a host of other things that are not looked at holistically. So I think the problem is the lack of a holistic perspective in that sense. We're targeting the surface symptoms and not the root problem.

'IT'S YOUR FAULT YOU DIDN'T TAKE CARE OF YOURSELF.'

MK

Interesting. What are some of the mental health, or even suicide-related stigmas in the lower-income groups?

Ying Jia

Even in general mental health, especially in society, we think that things happen because it's the individual's fault. You don't have enough self-control. You're not disciplined enough, and that's why these things happen to you. So I think it's something that has been drilled into us since young, especially in Asian families. If you don't do well, it's your fault—you didn't study hard enough. So if you fall into depression, it's your fault—you didn't take care of yourself or you just didn't have the self-discipline to get yourself out of it. So lots of these things prevent people from talking about issues that they might face because people might just tell you that you need to get yourself together, and there's no support or greater understanding.

But the thing is all these problems are very common. It's just that people are afraid to speak up. For example, in one of the programs that we have, we're trying to facilitate safe conversations among parents to talk about the issues they face raising kids. So at first, all of them were very quiet, and no one wanted to speak up. But once we as facilitators shared our own personal stories and problems we were facing at home, we realized that the pace actually picked up and a lot of people were sharing more openly. So it's not that they weren't facing problems but that they were afraid to speak up because it might seem that they are incapable of raising their kids.

MK

How do you think the general community is coping with that?

Ying Jia

I think a lot of people might not necessarily share these things, even on a day-to-day basis when they're speaking to their friends. There are a lot of unhelpful coping strategies in Singapore, even pre-COVID or during COVID currently. That might be how people actually try to cope because there's no other outlet. They can't really speak openly about their problems, so they have to find other ways to cope with it. Even during COVID, what we hear from the family service centres and news outlets is that there's an increase in family violence because there's just no space for them to handle and cope with their stress, so they have to take it out somewhere and they end up taking it out on their families.

MK

Are there any other mental health stigmas you have observed in your work?

Ying Jia

I noticed that when we define people by their household income—for instance, low-income groups with a household income of $2,500 and below—we're actually neglecting this other group of not so well-to-do families that don't qualify for any of the government assistance. We call them the sandwiched families.

MK

What do you mean by sandwiched families?

Ying Jia

Most of them are around their thirties or forties. They have children to take care of as well as their elderly parents with quite a bit of health conditions. They're sandwiched because they're responsible for taking care of those two generations, and although they are not financially poor, they are also not financially well-to-do enough to actually take care of so many dependents, which results in a lot of stress for them, and these are not really recognized. For example, there are limited help schemes for this population group despite the ground evidence or stories from centres that these are the problems they are facing. It's just not recognized because the criteria is fixated on financial capability. So what we're noticing is a unique, relatively new thing that hasn't really surfaced in other more matured areas. These families are actually very stressed, and most of these stresses are family related.

MK

Because they're dealing with survival conversations where money is not enough?

Ying Jia

Money is not enough, and they have so many relational problems to take care of.

MK

It's basically beyond their capacity.

Ying Jia

They're definitely working way beyond their capacity, both at work and in their personal life.

WE NEED TO BE A KINDER SOCIETY

MK

Got it. What are some of the things that have been done to alleviate the current circumstances that we're in?

Ying Jia

Okay, so because this is quite a new group, although we have anecdotal evidence, we know things cannot roll out unless there's concrete evidence to show that there's a real need. So actually there's no support from the government for these people because they just don't qualify for any of these existing services. For example, they can only receive some form of counselling, but because most of these people are working full-time in order to support their families, they often just don't even turn up for their counselling appointments. So although they have access to help, they don't have the means to get it. So I can say that, yes, there are available services like the usual counselling services, but the main issue is them being unable to even receive these services because of the circumstances that they're in.

MK

What more do you think can be done?

Ying Jia

Outside of the work context, I personally feel that we need to have more empathy for the individual. Everyone's going through their own struggles, but we tend to judge first. Because when I scroll through social media, maybe it's an article about suicide or an article about family violence, just look at the comments, they're just so lacking in empathy. They're just treating this as something that's not of their immediate concern, sort of like their separate bubble that they just watch and comment on, which I feel doesn't help. Because society is generally not understanding, and if there's no understanding, then who's gonna step up? We can't always depend on the government lah, we really need ground-up approaches, even just outside of work, even voluntary stuff to do. We need to be a kinder society. We are oftentimes too judgmental, although we ourselves might be going through struggles as well.

So both self-judgement as well as judgement onto others. I feel these are things that require a lot of time to tackle because it's so ingrained in us already.

So we need to change our perspective both at work and on a personal level. We can't just see it as it's that person's problem, it's not my problem because I'm not facing that. Everyone should be working together to solve certain things because as I mentioned, from the social media comments, you can clearly see that they're dividing themselves from others. There's a me versus them, their problem versus my problem, kind of worldview. We need to be more understanding and aware.

I think we judge because we don't even have the basic awareness of what's going on. We think that mental health conditions are the person's fault when really, it's a whole host of things, from a biopsychosocial point of view. And from COVID, we can already see that just an external stressor is enough to cause a whole society to have an increase in mental health conditions. I feel that that in itself is creating awareness that no one is necessarily safe from getting a mental health condition, and if we're just more aware, a bit more understanding about these things, then I think we can have a lot more safer and open conversations on a day-to-day basis.

FINDING OUT 7 YEARS LATER

MK

Anything else you want to add?

Ying Jia

Can I share from my personal experiences?

MK

Sure.

Ying Jia

I have a group of friends that I've known for ten years. I wouldn't say we're super close, but we do share things with each other. It was only recently that I learnt that about seven years ago, two of them contemplated committing suicide. I was completely unaware and didn't even suspect it because they are such happy people, and I only found out about this after they shared this seven years later. I feel like even within personal groups, there's so much that we don't know. It's really a lot more common than we think. So why is it that we can't have conversations about this when it's not an uncommon thing? It's not a weird thing at all too.

And I think they were only okay to share now because they're much better already. They're no longer in that state. So it's like, this bad thing happened which caused me to become good, that's why it's okay to share because there was a good outcome. But the thing is there are a lot of suicide cases where it just ends there—there was no good that came out of it. So we really need to talk about it starting now—not seven years later, not how many years later. We need to talk about it in the moment or even before they even begin thinking about committing suicide.

We really don't know our close friends enough because even we ourselves are afraid to be judged by them, because we don't know whether they will judge us or not. So yeah, just some thoughts. No conclusion yet, but . . . Yeah.

MK

When you first knew that your friends contemplated suicide, how did you feel? How did you deal with it?

Ying Jia

But they told me seven years later, so it was—

MK

It was a shock lah.

Ying Jia

It was definitely a shock because of all people, I wouldn't have expected them to be the ones. So it was a shock, and also a bit of guilt that I wasn't—

MK

Able to support them.

Ying Jia

I just assumed things. They looked happy, so there was no need to specially ask about them, so I felt guilty.

MK

You didn't see it coming.

Ying Jia

Yeah. I don't even know how we got to the topic, but they just mentioned it. But I was so relieved after that, that they were still here.

MK

One of the things that we need to do as a collective is that all the more, we have to speak out the truth. All the more we have to speak about the unsaid because it is the unsaid that kills people. The more we don't talk about these things, the more there isn't clarity or light around it.

Ying Jia

And the more we talk about it, the more other people will be willing to talk about it.

MK

So it's really about creating openness for people so that we can explore these themes in a clearer frame and begin to open up conversations. I think it's time for us to look into this because it has taken too many lives.

Ying Jia

Lots of things to do. We just need to be kind to each other. We don't have to wait for someone to be down before we start caring for them. We can always care about them on a day-to-day basis.

CHAPTER TEN

There Must Be a Better Way to Live

By Josephine Chia-Teo, Co-founder, Insightful Training & Consultancy Pte Ltd

Josephine spent thirteen years in the public service sector helping unemployed persons upskill and find new jobs. However, it was not just an employment problem she was dealing with. She witnessed first-hand the emotional strain and stress retrenched or unemployed individuals had to deal with on a daily basis, and how their emotional outlook had a negative impact on their job search.

THERE IS NO QUICK FIX

Si Qi

Can you tell me more about your mental health journey?

Josephine

I spent about thirteen years in the public service sector working with people who are unemployed. And these individuals face many mental health issues because anyone who is unemployed, going through retrenchment, or looking for a job, goes through a lot, be it mentally, physically, or emotionally. I was front facing in my line of work, so I saw a lot of people. Especially in the last five years, there were a lot more people who got retrenched or couldn't find work after they quit because of their age. And Singapore is an aging population, right? So we have a lot of people who are over the age of forty, and it is very demoralizing and disappointing to know that some employers really discriminate by age and gender.

If you're over forty, you are considered old. Even before employers see you, they will do a phone interview and the first thing they will ask you is how old are you? And there's no way to avoid this question. People are constantly getting reminded of the fact that they're aging, they're going to be irrelevant in the workforce, they're going to be paid less, and all that. So there are all these issues that job seekers face.

Si Qi

And your job was to help them get employed again?

Josephine

Yes, what we did was to try to help them upskill. That means we find their gaps. Let's say that I've been retrenched from the construction industry. And of course, construction is not booming right now and I won't be able to find a similar job. So what we do is to look for their skill gaps. Maybe they want to go into IT, for example. What are the skills they're lacking? How do they present themselves? How can they rewrite their resume? These are the gaps we help them to bridge so it makes their interview process easier.

But then you realize that even with all these 'cosmetic things' that we do, the individual still might not get the job or even the interview. There is a lot of mental pressure. And these people send out a lot of resumes. First month, second month, third month, you don't get a callback, it's fine. But it takes its toll on you when you still don't get a callback after six to nine months. There are some candidates I've talked to who only got called three times for an interview in nine months. They start to think what's wrong with me? In Singapore, we classify them as long-term unemployed persons if they have been unemployed for approximately six months or longer.[9] All these labels will add on to their mental stress. And because a lot of them are in their mid-forties, they probably have just started their families so they have an added financial stress.

I've met this guy before, early forties, second child was just born. He was in retail, and retail is an industry where you think you can find work easily, right? But he was a retail manager and earning quite a good salary, something like $8,000. He couldn't find any jobs and he had gone for more than ten interviews. So he would call me up every day and tell me I cannot find money to pump patrol, my wife is nagging at me, asking me when I'm going to find a job. He leaves the house everyday dressed, pretending he is going for interviews when in fact he's just loitering outside and coming to see me if I'm free, just to have somebody to talk to. But these are people who will not go to IMH to get help because there is that mark there if you've been there. So there are so many types of pressures that are unseen, and I feel for them. All they can do is to call career coaches like us,

[9] Manpower Research & Statistics Department, "Long-Term Unemployment Rate and Number Concepts and Definitions," Labour Market Statistics and Publications, https://stats.mom.gov.sg/SL/Pages/Long-Term-Unemployment-Level-and-Rate-Concepts-and-Definitions.aspx

but because I have so many people to serve on a daily basis, I cannot spend all my time with one person and talk to him for hours. I can only do my best to listen for twenty minutes and then I have to tell him I'm so sorry sir, but I really have to go. So where do they go? Who do they talk to? In the end, they just keep spiraling downwards emotionally. At the end, if they hit the bottom and they do not seek help, that's when your divorce cases go up, your child abuse cases go up, your domestic violence cases go up.

In the service, we try to give mental resilience talks. But these talks only address the surface issues. They teach a person how to look out for signs that they're mentally stressed. But so what? If I can check off a list that says that I'm mentally stressed, does that give me reprieve that I will get financial aid, or I will have money to buy milk powder for my kids next month? No. So even if they know they are in a mentally unhealthy state, that they might have depression, anxiety, and all that, they don't do anything about it because there is no motivation for them to do so. There is also no reward at the end where they can say if I get help, I will definitely get a job next month. All they want is to find work, so they keep going for interviews. But because they're already mentally distressed, their performance gets worse with every interview they go to. In the end, no employer will call them. So it's very real. If you ask me if there is a quick fix for mental health issues, there's no quick fix.

I JUST WANT TO RETURN TO A PEACEFUL HOME

Josephine

There are public mental health programmes out there that help with the lower economic class, but how about those that are stuck in between? The middle class and upper middle class are the sandwiched classes. Because they have a condo, they have a car, they're stuck with mortgage and car repayments when they lose their jobs. If they could sell their house or car, they would, but they can't because they've still got outstanding loans, which means they will still have to fork out the money to repay the loans that they've taken. So they're just stuck!

As a career coach, my own mental health gets affected as well because some clients are verbally abusive when they meet me. They're like what do you mean you can't help me? Why can't you help me? I need a job, just match me with a job. So as front-facing workers, we are very stressed as well. Do we have an outlet? No. Because it's an ongoing thing. We see up to eight clients a day.

Si Qi

Wow, eight people in a day is a lot . . .

Josephine

It's a lot. And let's say, even if half are not verbally abusive, they still come in with their emotional problems. By the time work ends, you're so mentally drained that you just can't wait to go home so you can have your peace for the rest of the day. And if you don't know how to draw the lines, you end up bringing all your mental stress home.

I have two young girls, and I would always shout at them for the last couple of years. This was what led me to quit the service. I go home after work feeling so drained. And when I go home, my kids want to talk to me, my spouse wants to talk to me. But I don't want to talk because my speech quota for the day has been met. Then the weekend comes and I still just want to have my own time. It defeats the purpose of starting a family. So I said no, the mental health of my children and my family is more important.

At the end of the day, it was very hard to bear because I was already bordering on anxiety issues. I came home and my kids were jumpy. I don't know if you believe in it, but our energy bounces off others and it affects the people around us.

Si Qi

Yeah, I do.

Josephine

Right. So my kids get affected by my anxious energy the minute I return home. They will be screaming at each other, asking to watch TV or to eat ice cream at seven in the evening when they're supposed to be in bed an hour later. I wanted to come home to my loving family, yet I came home to even more chaos. I found myself screaming at them, hitting them, and all that. Eventually I said to myself, what am I doing? This has to stop. That's why I quit the service in 2019 after thirteen years. A lot of my ex-colleagues and friends are still there.

Si Qi

And COVID has worsened the job market, right?

Josephine

Yeah, so they come to me and they say 'Josephine, I know you're running some mental resilience programmes with your partner who's a psychologist. Can you help us run a programme so that internally, we have our own support system?' Because they have no time to go for training, no time to see a counsellor too. You see, we don't get our own mental health checked at all. The only thing we could do was complain to colleagues. For example, after meeting a particularly difficult client, we can have a debrief session with each other. But most of the time, we don't do it properly. We just complain and all the negativity stays there. It doesn't get resolved. Nobody helps you process your feelings, things like how are you feeling? Here's how you can let go of the negative feelings for this client. There was no such process for us. That's why many frontline workers are feeling very burnt out.

IS THERE A WAY OUT?

Si Qi

You were in a position where you met people who are in distress because a basic financial and material need of theirs was not met.

I can understand the dilemma from your story. On one hand, they are in need of mental health support, but at the same time their basic needs need to be met too. Which comes first?

Josephine

Correct. It's a chicken or egg question. Just . . . Wow . . . When you see the same job seeker month after month, your heart really goes out to them. They are willing to drop their expectations to take a $3,000 job. They are willing to do anything, even anything administrative. But even an administrator needs certain skill sets which they don't have. Let's say you're a retail manager and you don't have admin skills. Even if you're willing to lower your position, people might not hire you.

Especially for people who are above the age of forty-five, it takes a longer time to find a job. So we try to manage our clients' expectations by telling them that it may take nine months to a year and a half to find a job, and they were like, but I don't have savings to last that long. And I was like wait but you're living in a condo? So they cannot ask for financial assistance. If they go to any social service office and say I need to put food on the table, I need financial assistance, people will look at your address and if it's a condo or landed property, you don't get any help. These people are really left hanging there. I can understand how frustrated they must feel.

Si Qi

How do you think we can start to tackle this issue in society? I think from your story, it's clear that mental health is interconnected with so many other things, it's not just solely about your mental state. How do we address the stigma with mental health? Is there a way out for us?

Josephine

Yes, there is a way out of our current problem, and that is to start planning your career path earlier. Many people get complacent.

They feel that their job is forever, so they don't have a concrete career plan. They don't think about things like what if I get laid off next month? Do I have enough savings to last me for six months to one year? Many people spend their paycheck without saving. There are some people I've met who don't have savings to last them even three months! And some of them have a car and a maid. What happens for them is that they spend most of their paycheck every month. It's the reality.

So it's about education. We need to go upstream to educate people who are in their late thirties or early forties to start planning for retirement. We also need to educate people to start career planning the moment they enter the workforce. You must constantly be aware of your market value and the industry that you're in. You need to be aware of the fact that you can get replaced by somebody who is younger and cheaper, which is the reality of things. We have to start planning early.

For example, if you foresee that your job will stay relevant only for the next twenty years tops, do you start thinking about what you can do after you're forty? Most of us don't, right? We maybe only think about whether we can stay in our current position for the next three years. But we need to have a long-term plan that goes together with our life stages. Are you going to get married? When you start a family, are you going to continue working? As a woman, are you going to have kids? When you have kids, childcare issues come up too. All these things need to be planned for.

These types of planning are inevitable. If you don't have any financial stress and you can live day-to-day, that's fine. But you must also know where your threshold for stress is. That's why my partner and I came up with this programme called the Pause Coach. It's about knowing where your threshold for stress is. If on the scale of one to ten, your threshold for stress is six, which means you feel very overwhelmed when you reach six-and-a-half, then you should start planning earlier and start learning what stresses you out before you hit your threshold.

A CONSCIOUS WAY OF LIVING

Si Qi

I think the importance of living true to who you are is showing up very strongly through your sharing. What is the life you want to lead? Sometimes we can be a bit disconnected from that idea because there are so many external expectations that we think we need to fulfil, like oh I must buy a condo to impress my wife. I must buy a luxury car to impress my friends and relatives. These external expectations are constantly tugging and pulling us in all different directions, away from our personal responsibility to ourselves, away from the need to be true to ourselves first and foremost. And if we are not responsible for and true to ourselves, it would create problems for other people as well.

In the case of mental health, how do we build that responsibility and connection to the self?

Josephine

Mindfulness is a very conscious effort that whatever you do at every stage of your life, you are mindful and conscious of the decision that you're making. So when I quit my job, I also have to be mindful that the stress is going to be on my husband. Of course, you have to communicate with each other . . . I didn't just quit out of the blue just because I couldn't take it anymore and therefore sorry, you have to shoulder the responsibility of being the sole breadwinner. We talked about it. So there is the communication bit that you need to talk to the people that you're responsible for as well.

But it really all boils down to having a more conscious way of living. Even the way we eat, the way we use things, we're destroying the earth's resources. We can start by being more conscious with our use of plastics, for example. It's really about being conscious of the choices you make at every moment. It's tough, it's a very tall order, but there's no other way about it.

There has to be education about consciousness. Which means not just living every day in our comfort zone, not just doing everything blindly and taking for granted that every day is going to be the same. If I buy a drink, can I make the choice to bring my own straw? That is a conscious effort to save the planet. Can I choose to recycle and be sustainable for a week? That is a conscious effort. If I want to save money today, can I choose to ignore the online sales?

[Josephine laughs]

Josephine

So it's about consumerism too. Can I not be influenced by peer pressure, external factors, or marketing? So not going to the office has actually been a good reprieve for a lot of people because you don't see your colleagues. But when you go back to work and your colleagues are eating at this expensive restaurant, you would want to follow along because you want to have that social interaction. If your colleagues carry a Prada bag, you might start thinking maybe I could buy a Prada bag too since I didn't travel this year. But with a conscious way of living, you would start asking yourself things like do I need more bags at home? What can I do with this money? Can I save or invest it? It's about being mindful of every single decision that you make. Does it serve your purpose? Then it comes to the question of what is your purpose, right? That is a very big question. Everything is interconnected.

Si Qi

Yeah, and the topic of mental health does lead us to these fundamental questions. What do you want to do? What's your purpose? Who are you? It's not easy to answer and therefore, I suppose that's why mental health and these tough questions can be very confronting for some.

Josephine

So people rather just not think about it. And one day it will come back, and the issue would have become so big that you can't avoid it. It'll hit you like a bus.

Si Qi

And you've seen it firsthand.

Josephine

Yeah, nine out of ten of my clients come in and look like they got hit by a bus.

Si Qi

I feel your story in my stomach. It's just . . . Gut wrenching. It's horrible.

Josephine

It's horrible. And people have asked me can I get your job, how do I get your job? And you can just tell how desperate they are when they even ask you a question like that. Your heart will go out to them. There were many times I cried with my clients because I can feel what they're going through; they have kids and all that too. But I can't help. I can't loan them money. I can't do all that because I've got my own family too. I can only offer that space for them, yet I can't give them too much time because I have my next appointment to go to.

So that's why I think it's important that we treat each other more like human beings rather than just a client relationship. Maybe if we gave them the time and space to air things out, they would not feel so constricted. And they would feel better and more motivated to look for jobs after the session with the coach.

PARENTING IS A SKILL

Si Qi

So on the topic of education, we know from the mental health space that a lot of issues are passed down from generations the kind of mindset, values, and even emotions. How can parents start to educate themselves so that they can educate their kids better?

Josephine

Have you heard of the conscious parenting movement?

Si Qi

Tell me more.

Josephine

Okay so when your child acts up right, let's say your child stole something. Of course as a parent, you will berate your child, 'Why did you steal, stealing is no good, blah blah blah'.

But what's beneath the stealing behaviour? This child might be stealing in order to get attention from the family. Maybe both parents are working and the child is left at home with the helper, which is very common in Singapore these days. Any kind of attention is better than no attention from a child's perspective. I want to be seen. So the conscious thing for parents to do is to ask why is my child stealing? What made him steal? After that, talk to the child in a way that doesn't shame him or her.

Conscious parenting teaches us to take some time to understand what is going on beneath that behaviour. What are your children trying to tell you? Children are not able to verbalize what they're feeling. Sometimes they don't even have the vocabulary for their emotions, only happy or sad. Even adults have limited emotional vocabulary. We only know happy, sad, angry, but there are so many other emotions.

What we could also do is teach parents to reflect on their child's behaviour, because our children will reflect our subconscious. My eldest daughter is very angsty all the time. When I first started learning about mindfulness, I couldn't help but scold her all the time and say things like I'm going to cane you if you don't stop shouting. But as I went along with my practice, I asked myself, why am I so angsty? And I realized it's my job. I'm always angsty at work, and my children reflect that behaviour at home. All of their behaviours are learned. If it's not from the TV, it's learned behaviour from the childcare centre, or from the extended family. From the way they eat, the way they behave, to the way they dress—everything is learned. You need to be conscious enough to know that the 'negative traits' that your child possess are usually a reflection of a behaviour you exhibit, a behaviour the people around them exhibit, or even something that society deems as bad. In truth, there are no good or bad behaviours, just behaviours. It's what's underneath that's more important.

The conscious parenting movement is very hard for many parents to swallow because they might think I've always been a hardworking girl at school. I don't know why my child is so lazy. If you have a certain judgement towards laziness, your child portraying such traits would trigger that judgement in you. If she's lazy, then she's lazy; you don't need to label it. And when we try to understand what's beneath the laziness, we might find that she could just be tired after school. We don't see what she does in school, yet we immediately say things like hey why are you so lazy? Can you pick up your shoes? Can you do this, can you do that. All the labelling comes in. But if you really take the conscious effort to self-reflect, you'll see that your child mirrors the kind of behaviour that you've been exhibiting all along, whether it's at work or at home. Your child is just showing you things that you are not willing to face about yourself.

Si Qi

Right.

Josephine

So I learn a lot from my kids. I tell you, my kids really show me what an ugly person I am.
[Josephine laughs]

Josephine

And I thank them for being that. But many parents are not willing to face that because it's very confronting, and they've already got so much stress at work. They don't want to come back home to see their kids show them what kind of person they are. So they stuff phones, tablets, and laptops in front of their kids. When you see families eating out, what do the kids usually have in front of them? A handphone. That's the only way to keep them quiet. Then you wonder why the kids are not engaged, why they have a very short attention span, why they get bored very easily. In the beginning when I was raising my kids, they were very noisy at restaurants. So what did we do? We stopped going out to eat.
[Josephine laughs]

Josephine

Because we realized that as parents, we were going out because we needed to go out, we wanted to go to that hip café. But my daughter didn't want to be there. She threw tantrums when we were out, and you feel so embarrassed. As you're screaming at the kid you think to yourself: who wanted to go out? It was me!

So that was a phase. We stopped going out because it can be very embarrassing when the kids are shouting and basically doing what kids do. They'll play, drop cutlery, break things and all that, and people will be looking at you like hey what kind of parent are you. I mean, I don't want to be judged too.

Si Qi

There's so much judgement, right? Just in our everyday lives, there's a lot of judgement from people around us, which ultimately is connected to mental health because you are being judged for who you are and what you're doing without the full context of you as a person. So why would you go and confront any of your deeper personal issues? Why would you confront it if it's labelled as you're not good enough as a parent? Why would you go and do something about it when it's something shameful to admit?

So how can we start to address these kinds of stigmas in society?

Josephine

Be honest with yourself. Parenting is not an art. It's a skill. It's something that you need to learn. Nobody becomes a mother overnight. You can have the baby, but you don't know what to do with it. And everybody feels the same, but nobody wants to talk about it.

You see on Instagram how people brag about their children. But they don't talk about the things that their children don't do well in because it's shameful; because they don't like others to see their flaws. But that is human nature. We falter and it's okay to make mistakes. Yet society does not allow us to fail, so we only present the best sides of ourselves on social media.

I stopped looking at Facebook because of the peer pressure there. You see this perfect parent with this bento set for her kid that contains every other thing on the food pyramid.
[laughter]

And I'm giving my kid bread and biscuits. I start to compare. But where is this getting me? It's just making me feel lousy about myself. So I start by detoxing, and when I feel mentally and emotionally stronger, I can then appreciate this person and her post without comparing myself to it. But I'm not there yet, so I'll continue with detoxing first.

When you are a novice at mindfulness and conscious living, you will fail many times. You need to start by getting rid of all the hindrances and distractions first, build yourself up, and become a little bit more powerful internally. Then you can start to reintegrate to the external world.

People always think that mindfulness means you need to go to a remote place in the mountains to practice it. But no, it's the small things that you do every day. You can remove the distractions, but you still have to live your life, and the life we live in is the practice ground. If you don't feel so strong on certain days, just retreat into your sanctuary first. But most people don't even have a sanctuary to retreat to.

Si Qi

That is very true. That is very true, which is the whole problem right, so—

Josephine

So what do we do? We compensate by shopping when we are mentally stressed. Even for myself, I go onto social media, I look at shopping sites, thinking that it will just numb the mind. But it doesn't get rid of the noise, it just shuts it off for a while. Then when you go back to your daily life you realize it comes back again.

WE'RE ALL FRIENDS HELPING FRIENDS

Si Qi

My next question is this. You have met a lot of people from your previous job who come to you at a state where everything is crashing down on them at the same time. And that is usually the time when people start seeking help or external support for their mental health. It's usually when something big happens, like the loss of a family member, a major illness, or the loss of a job. But we know that by then, intervention can be more challenging because you have so many things you're trying to solve at the same time. So how do we encourage people to start on the conscious living bandwagon earlier than later?

Josephine

It's never too late. One of my teachers in a mindfulness course told me that it's never too late to have a happy childhood. However crappy your life is, the minute you make the decision to start to be more mindful, then that's it.

Of course, when you talk about job seekers, they are in a dire position. What they can do is to make that conscious effort, that full commitment that today, I'm going to look for work, I'm going to pick myself up. You start from there. The problem is that not everybody will be supportive and understanding of your situation. People say yeah you see lah, you wait until like that then find solution. So your support system has to be very strong. Mix with people who are more positive. Maybe you can do some volunteer work, do something that is meaningful, and surround yourself with people who will not judge you for the state that you are in. People who can say it doesn't matter how you got there. I don't care how you became bankrupt, or how you got into this state I'm not going to judge you. I see you for who you are. Let's move forward. You need to surround yourself with people like that. That is my advice for people who are currently in a very jialat situation. There's nothing much we can do but go upwards.

Si Qi

And if there's one message you want to say to people about mental health, what would that be?

Josephine

That we're all friends helping friends. That has always been my line. I am not your counsellor, I'm not your coach. I'm just your friend. I'm a fellow human being who happens to be in a better position to help you. And I always remind myself that I have to be a friend to myself too. If I can't help myself, I can't help somebody else.

We're here to help each other. I'm not better than you. We have our challenges and we're just helping each other along the way in this thing called life, which is not a very long span of time. We just need to stop judging other people, whether good or bad. If we could just see each other as human beings, I think the world, even just Singapore, will be a much better place. Everybody's equal.

CHAPTER ELEVEN

The Complexities of Mental Health at Old Age

By Nur Farhan Bte Mohammad Alami, Geriatrician, Raffles Medical Group

The disruptions to our daily routines during COVID-19 hit some elderly people much harder, as their sources of meaning and purpose from their routines were abruptly removed from them. Farhan shares that elderly people usually have a harder time dealing with stresses in life, largely because they are less physically resilient as well. In order for us to all prepare for old age, and to age gracefully, education about maintaining one's health and wellness has to start young so that we can enjoy our older years.

WHAT WE SEE IS JUST THE TIP OF THE ICEBERG

Farhan

I'm a geriatrician, which means I see older people. I regularly treat depression and dementia in older people.

MK

Let's zoom in on that. What are some of the major trends you're seeing today?

Farhan

Right now, we are in a pandemic, and people from vulnerable populations are hit in various ways with regards to isolation and difficulty in accessing their usual day to day activities. For example, daycare centres are closed, and their social circles have become smaller. I have older patients who have lost their jobs because of the economy. I have older people who are regular volunteers but because of COVID, they are told that they are vulnerable to getting infected, so they are not allowed to come in to do their usual volunteer work. So it's quite tough because an older person needs to feel relevant. They need to have purpose, otherwise it affects their psyche and it can get very difficult for them.

They can be coping perfectly well. For example, I had an older patient, an eighty-year-old lady who was not allowed to enter her grandchild's school anymore. She was a volunteer in the school library where she did a lot of work with regards to engaging the children, stock-taking, rearranging books, and when that stopped, she started to feel like there's no reason for her to remain living. So she ended up drinking a lot of alcohol and when she was found one morning by her daughter on the floor, she discovered that she had suffered a fracture in her spine. She ended up in the hospital where there were a lot of complications which included things like infections, confusion, and difficulty walking. When she came out from the hospital, she was not in a good state at all.

MK

That's a lot of food for thought.

Farhan

Yes. I mean, we always say that what you see is just the tip of the iceberg. So if you see an older patient with a fall in the hospital, that's just the tip of the iceberg because you can see that she fell, was found on the floor, but there were a lot of other things going on.

MK

Internally.

Farhan

And also physically. What we mean by tip of the iceberg is that there really is so much going on underneath that a lot of times we struggle to bring them back to their pre-fall state, or their original state. It's not like a younger person where there's resilience, in a way, not just mental or emotional, but physical reserves. If you look at an older person, we always describe them as frail. Some older people are frail, and what it actually means is that they have a decrease in responses to stressors. You stress them out, they just cannot *tahan*.[10] Not all older people are frail, but frail older people end up being a lot of the people I work with.

Si Qi

What are some of these stresses that affect older people more?

---

[10] Tahan: Local slang for tolerate

Farhan

Okay, so when I say stressors, I mean physical stressors. Like if we have a cough or cold, I mean, why does the COVID mortality rate disproportionately skew towards older people? If a young person catches COVID, for example, there is a higher chance of recovery. But if you are above seventy-five years old, your risk of death can be ten times higher. So this is what I mean by them not having the physical reserves to fight diseases or infections. And these stressors are not mental and emotional, but they can also be mental and emotional. For example, if we fracture an arm, we're still able to dress ourselves, we're still able to go to work. But when an older person breaks their arm, they cannot dress themselves, they cannot bathe on their own, and just by having one arm immobilized, their risk of fall increases. So this is an example of them not being able to cope with it. When I say stressors, a lot of times, it means physical illness.

MK

Got it. So how does that contribute and lead to depression?

Farhan

It's not direct. I wouldn't say that somebody will fall and become depressed.

You know your body and mind are linked, right? So for example, stroke, a disease of older people. If you have a stroke, depression is considered a comorbidity, which means it tends to come together. Another example would be smoker's lung, which just means you've been smoking for a long time and you get this sort of end-stage lung disease. So if you have these conditions, your chances of getting depression are higher. I wouldn't say that a fall will lead to depression, but if you accumulate a lot of physical illness which happens as you age, then your risk of having mood issues and depression is higher. Make sense?

MK

Definitely. It makes sense. I'm just wondering, you know, for the elderly, at least from your experience, what are the statistics of the people who are depressed?

Farhan

So it ranges, but I would say about 10 per cent or even higher, depending on what sort of data you look at.

MK

This is based in Singapore or globally?

Farhan

Well, I don't know the statistics outright. I cannot quote, but I would say that 10 per cent is what we usually see. Some studies can show up to 20 per cent.

THE SILVER TSUNAMI

MK

Got it, got it. And as you know, we are an aging population.

Farhan

Yes, of course. One in four Singaporeans will be above the age of sixty-five in 2030. So we're going to see a silver tsunami we're talking about close to 1,000,000 people. So then if 10 per cent is considered high right, you will have like 100,000 above sixty-five who may experience depression.

MK

This is going to be a major problem, considering that right now, even as youth ourselves, there is still a lack of understanding of what mental health is. There's still so much stigma and that ignorance is going to follow us throughout the years.

Farhan

Definitely, yeah. When I talk about dementia, there's so much stigma as well, in terms of memory and forgetfulness. When you talk to older people, because older people are concerned about their memory right, it's actually quite difficult to reach out to them because in these times, so much of what we're doing are online events.

I met someone who said that you really should go younger to the Instagram generation, not the Facebook-ers. We should be educating the younger Instagram generation, like you and I. But we should also go further down to the TikTok generation, that's how you can create change. That's how you create awareness from down below. It's what we call a life course approach, where you don't just try to maintain your memory when you're sixty-five, but you should also be increasing your level of education because that protects you against dementia. Dementia awareness or dementia prevention should happen throughout your life from the time you were born. So I do agree that when you only think about depression when you're older, it's really, really difficult to change your mindset. You should be aware of what are mental health issues, and destigmatize it, like we do with youths.

Si Qi

For young adults, we know that typical external factors like work-related or financial stress could result in mental health issues like depression and anxiety. What are the external environmental factors that may cause mental health issues for older people?

Farhan

It's more or less the same. If you ask them what's stressing them out, it's always family, relationships, and finances. I mean, it's so difficult to get people to seek help or take medications when they're too poor to even get food, you see. And of course, physical illnesses. If you're in pain, and you don't sort that out, then of course you are going to be very sad and depressed.

Sometimes you'll be so shocked or surprised. When I asked this eighty-year-old lady why are you sad? Her reply was that my son fell down the stairs when he was ten years old and he died. And this is an eighty-year-old lady. Then you realize that that tragedy happened sixty years ago, and she was perfectly functional and well, raised the other ten children, but suddenly when she's eighty and coming to the end of life, she's depressed because she never got over her son's death. Those things really shock me sometimes.

Older people have a lot of experiences, but they also have lots of tragedies. They have wisdom, they have good things that happen to them, but they also have emotional baggage. If you are twenty or thirty years old and you have emotional baggage, then by eighty, you have a huge baggage. So it's complex, the things that bother them. But it doesn't mean that they are not forthcoming. If you ask them something, a lot of times they have a lot of things to say.

MK

The thing is, you know, people always think that time heals all wounds. But we all know that is not true.

Farhan

Yes, you just sweep it under the rug.

MK

Yeah. But it comes back and haunts us.

Farhan

Exactly. Totally.

DEALING WITH MULTIPLE LOSSES AT AN OLD AGE

MK

What do you think is really causing all these issues that are surfacing at a later age?

Farhan

A lot of times, there's a lot of loss as they get older. They lose their spouse, they may outlive their children, outlive their brothers and sisters, and their parents are definitely long gone. So it's loss, loss, and more loss. Then when they have a fall and cannot walk, they lose function, lose independence, it just feels like there's more and more to grief, I suppose.

Si Qi

Yeah. And what do you think are some of the mental health stigmas that prevent older people from seeking help?

Farhan

Well, I suppose they may think that it's a normal part of aging. There are lots of symptoms of depression and one of them is a loss of the feeling of joy—we call it anhedonia—where you lose pleasure and everything. Older people may just think that this is a normal part of aging. I'm old already, I'm useless. It's like okay, I want to not do anything and this is just how it's gonna end. So perhaps a sense of helplessness.

WHAT DOES NORMAL AGING LOOK LIKE?

Si Qi

And what do you think we can do to support them better in receiving help?

Farhan

The first thing would be to realize that this is not normal. When an older person loses interest in everything, doesn't want to go out of the house, stops walking, stops talking, stops eating, stops sleeping, all these are signs that they are unwell. And it can be a physical illness, it can be mood-related, it can also be memory issues. It can be many things. So the first thing would be to not accept that normal aging involves being passive or losing interest or not leaving the household.

Si Qi

I think that's really true, because perhaps we have an idea from the media that when you age, you become more sedentary, and you just fade into the background of life. There are really a lot of stereotypes that come with how aging is supposed to look like.

Farhan

Yeah, and it's quite tough. Some of my patients, when they lose their hearing, they lose their eyesight, they just become more and more quiet, and they start to live in their own world because they cannot participate in conversations or don't really know what's going on. So then you wonder, are they depressed? Are they dementing? Are they physically sick? It's so hard to tell. And it's challenging for family members as well, because when they've got all these impairments, when they can't see you, when they can't hear you, it's just so easy to coexist and not interact. It takes much more effort to pull them in to engage them.

Si Qi

I think it's a challenge for family members because it gets very frustrating not being able to understand the seniors in their house. What can family members do to support their elderly better?

Farhan

I suppose the first thing I would say is that you are not alone. If you are a caregiver for an elderly person, which means you help them in areas where they cannot help themselves, that itself is a very challenging 24/7, 365-day role. So community matters. Talking to other people, especially those who have walked the path that you have. It's hard to do it alone and the caregivers themselves, family members of my patients, are prone to mental health issues as well. I mean you can imagine having to look after an elderly person who's having depression, for example, then on top of it there's physical illnesses and disabilities. It's been shown that caregivers are prone to depression and burnout. So the first step would be to look after yourself, to know that you're not alone, to network with other caregivers.

If you're doing everything, which includes running the household, looking after your own children, doing the housework, looking after an old person, then ask for help. Look for other support services which can be formal or informal. Don't think that you're alone and don't do it all alone. You need to prioritize yourself because the family is vulnerable.

Too depressing, right? I already feel so depressed, it's like . . . [Farhan laughs]

Farhan

As in, this conversation itself is all doom and gloom. We should try to put it in a more positive light.
[laughter]

Farhan

It's not so bad, right?

MK

Well, I don't think it's bad. I think this conversation is important. It's important that we understand what mental health is so that it doesn't spill over and affect us over time.

THERAPY DIDN'T EXIST IN THE OLDER GENERATIONS

MK

So, I'm just wondering, what are some measures we can implement to elevate or bring these issues to light to reduce what's happening in society?

Farhan

Well, firstly, it should be a national plan, right? To raise awareness of depression in the elderly, memory problems, and even the diagnosis of dementia in the elderly. It has to be a nationwide work plan. That would be how it should be.

But I suppose there's always a need to support advocacy groups, for example. To encourage people to have conversations and to reach out to older people in their lives. You have grandma, grandpa, grand uncle, grand aunty. On a macro level, it's the work of organizations at a national level, but then at a micro level–our level–it is really to reach out to our networks, our community, and that would have an impact on everyone.

Si Qi

I think sometimes older people can be very averse to any form of mental health help because they might think that *talking to people got use meh*? They can solve my problems meh? So how do we actually talk to them about mental health treatment?

Farhan

Exactly, it's really tough. I was reading a book written by a psychologist. It's called *Maybe You Should Talk To Someone* by Laurie Gottlieb. If you've not read this book, you should.

So it's by a psychologist about her psychologist. She was in her forties and she was about to get married when suddenly, her longtime partner said oh, by the way, I don't think I can marry you because you have a son. That sort of pushed her into therapy, and she talked about her journey. So in her book, she said that older people would never see a therapist because it didn't even exist in their time. In my experience, I find that it's true. When I suggest to my older patients to see a counsellor, they always look at me like are you crazy? You want me to sit down and pay someone to talk to me? So it's not unusual. And in this book, she pulled up data that showed that older people don't want to see a psychologist because it's really not in their generation. So, it's tough. It's tough.

I convince them by saying that it takes three to four to five therapies before you find the right fit. I actually had one patient who had seen someone and then she came back—she was eighty something—and she said oh, you know, I know more than him. He knows nothing.

Si Qi

I eat salt more than you eat rice, something like that?

Farhan

Exactly, exactly. And I'm like okay, maybe he's not the right fit and she's like what do you mean not the right fit? He has all these qualifications on his walls. He has a PhD in this, this, and this. No one else can be better. Don't make me see someone else.

But anyway, she ended up in the hospital and I managed to get someone else to see her. It seemed like a good fit. She liked this other therapist, and they're still doing therapy.

Si Qi

Right . . . It didn't even cross my mind that therapy probably didn't exist in our parents' generation.

OLDER PEOPLE CRAVE CONNECTIONS AND RELATIONSHIPS TOO

Si Qi

If you could leave the readers of this book with one message about mental health, what is something that you would like to say to them?
[silence]

Farhan

I would say that community matters. And that means maintaining your tribe, reaching out, and making connections with people. It's something that you may not do actively when you are trying to climb up in your career or you're busy raising a family, but nurturing relationships do matter.

And the other thing would be that there are so many older people around us. When was the last time you picked up the phone and called your grandma? We're always so busy, and it usually seems like there's not enough hours in the day, but it really goes a long way to make the effort to just check in with them. It does make them happy. Older people really crave connection and relationships. They are just as emotional, or even more emotional than us.

CHAPTER TWELVE

Do You See the Person First or the Disease First?

By Ng Jek Mui, Clinical Lead, Care Integration, Dementia Singapore (formerly known as Alzheimer's Disease Association)

As a professional caregiver for persons living with dementia, Jek Mui has developed a keen understanding and empathy towards their struggles, as well as the struggles of caregivers who more often than not, find themselves having to put their lives own hold for in order to fulfil their caregiving duties. In that regard, she shares some of the key elements that both persons living with dementia and caregivers need in order to create a healthier support system for themselves physically, mentally, and emotionally.

ENTERING INTO THEIR WORLD
AND THEIR REALITY

MK

Why don't you share with me more about what you do?

Jek Mui

My name is Jek Mui. Since 1 April 2021, I have moved from the Casework & Counselling team to the Care Integration team and a new role as the Clinical Lead at Dementia Singapore. To me, this is a new ground; it seems uncharted, yet at the same time, it feels like a consolidation of all my learnings, adaptations, and applications. An invitation to listen, explore, and understand from the many different people in this area of support. An opportunity to rethink, with a focus on the delivery of clinical services in dementia care, which includes persons with dementia and people impacted by dementia.

MK

Got it. For today's conversation on dementia, I want to understand the world inside the people living with dementia.

Jek Mui

Then you have to speak with someone who's living with dementia, because they are the experts of their lives!
[Jek Mui laughs]

MK

Correct. Right now, I don't have someone living with dementia, that's the truth. And I would want to understand what it's like from somebody who has spent a whole decade working with people living with dementia and their families.

Jek Mui

I think, first and foremost, the question is: do you see the person, or do you see the disease itself? So I think yes, we do refer to them as people living with dementia instead of people suffering from dementia. We are being very mindful and inclusive of the language and the choice of words that we use. With reference to 'Changing Words, Touching Lives', the appropriate language is, 'Respectful, Non-stigmatizing, Empowering, Accurate, Inclusive'.

I guess in a way, why I asked that question is because the one that you see first will set your perception, your attitude and mindset, feelings, and actions.

MK

Got it.

Jek Mui

So in supporting people living with dementia and caregivers, we look at the person first. And when we look at the person, we want to get to know the person by first establishing a relationship. We need to feel trusted, belonged, loved, that we matter, and that there is meaning. It takes time, patience, care, curiosity, interest, two-way interactions, and co-creation. To help us, we use the 'Enriched Model of Dementia' to understand their biography, health, personality, and the social psychology and environment. So, in a way, if you want to enter somebody's world—not just persons living with dementia, but any relationship—first you need to be invited. Meaning, you need to seek permission to enter, and entering itself involves vulnerability. It's not just you, who is entering the world, that is vulnerable, but the person who is allowing you to enter, is vulnerable as well. And the question is, are we able to hold each other in that space? It's this holding that sometimes makes it difficult, not just as a professional caregiver, but also as a family caregiver. It's difficult because it means that I have to know what you're going through, I need to feel the pain, I need to feel the hurt, and I also need to make a guess when you say you're confused or disoriented. What is it like?

When you asked me to share about persons living with dementia, the only closest thing I could think of was have you had days when you were sick and you've been so dosed with medication that you are very drowsy? It's almost like that because there is a lot of loss and confusion. You go to bed, you don't know what time it is, and you're wondering why am I not having my meal? I'm lethargic, I don't have energy. The other experience I can share is to think about travelling. Right now, of course we can't travel, but on days that we can, you'll feel that it's unfamiliar when you travel to a new place. You don't know what's out there. So persons with dementia are also trying to navigate their way. Even if they, in their biography, used to work in an airport and could travel from their home to where they work, over time, they may not be able to. And even when they do, they're not able to connect.

One of the examples I can think of is one of the ladies living with dementia. She used to stay in a kampong. She would often go out of the house alone because it's freedom for her, so she goes out and she always goes to the landed estate area because they all look like single-storey buildings. In her reality, that's a kampong, because it's single level. But for the people who live in the estate, it's like hm, why is this lady always coming by my house, knocking on my door? Another example is a male person living with dementia. He used to stay in a landed property, so every day in the afternoon, he'll go and knock on somebody's door. The unit is the same, but it's a different level. He does get confused. And it was through a lot of communication and sharing by the caregiver that the owner understood. Oh my dad actually has dementia and he used to stay in this house, so that's why he always frequents your place even when he's staying in an apartment now.

So if you were to say, for us without dementia, it's like travelling to an unfamiliar place and trying to navigate your way. Can you imagine that this is how they are living every day?

You may not know where you are when you wake up, because this is not the place that they used to wake up in, in the past. And they'll always tell you this is not my home, because to them in their reality many years ago, it's not their home. So the part about entering their reality is really about knowing the person, and what is important to them. And this needs time, patience, and a lot of understanding the person. That's also why caregiving for persons with dementia can be challenging or difficult, because caregivers may not know what they are like. If you're a child caregiver, you don't really know your parents' relationship. They may have fights and arguments, but you don't know why dad has to go out in the morning and come back in the evening. He doesn't talk to me at all, so why do I have to become a caregiver now? So there are a lot of family dynamics woven in as well.

Coming back to entering the reality of the person, we have to understand that because of dementia, the illness itself, they may not have the ability to remember events that just took place. What they have in their memory are long stored, fun, sad, happy moments that they have with different people. When you ask a question about recent events, it's challenging for them because they need to retrieve the answer. That's something we can do easily because our brain has not changed, and we are able to provide the answer instantly. But for them, they need to think, they need to process, they need to find the correct answer. For example, have you eaten? It's a very simple question that we will always ask each other. But for them, it's like, I ate, but what did I have? Why is it that I cannot remember what I ate? Why is this person even asking what I ate? So there will be more questions that come up, and because they may not have the ability to answer them or to find the answer, they will get frustrated and upset with themselves like why can't I even know whether I have eaten or not? So this upset, this frustration, is invisible to external parties.

MK

Got it.

Jek Mui

And to us, these responsive behaviours are a way of communicating their unmet needs. Personally, I can only imagine myself living with dementia, imagine being in their position, having to pick out whatever that is available to me in my mind, having to string it together to provide you an answer because I may feel obliged to answer you, since you are standing down there, sitting down there, waiting for an answer. I would feel very pressured, very anxious, like okay, did I answer correctly, or did I not? Even in school, we also feel that way when the teacher asks us questions. This almost sounds similar and can happen to anyone at some moment in time. We can 'move' out of that situation, as we have the abilities. So I guess for them, it's a challenge because they need to piece it together and when we hear it, it doesn't sound like a proper sentence.
[Jek Mui laughs]

Jek Mui

But I think most times, during the sessions that I have with persons living with dementia, it doesn't make sense at first. It really doesn't make sense, but when you know and understand their biography, who they are as a person, what path they have walked, then what they say begins to make sense.

YOU CAN WATCH BY THE RIVERBANK, OR FLOW WITH THE RIVER

MK

What kept you going after ten years? It takes a lot of tenacity to stay on in this field.

Jek Mui

How should . . .
[silence]

Well, first and foremost, I don't see it as a job *job*. So maybe that's why I just continued?
[Jek Mui laughs]

I think, first and foremost, what got me into social services was the desire to help people. Although there are ups and downs, like people not understanding, or funding issues—
[Jek Mui laughs]

Jek Mui

I think it's okay. Because whatever struggles that you have, at the end, it will pass. It's just at that moment, it's very critical, it's very glaring, and you want to do something about it. That's how we always feel when we are put into stressful situations, or into any situation that we don't like.

MK

Like issues that surface that make us lose control.

Jek Mui

I think as you talk about control . . . It's something that we all love and want to have. When things are beyond our control, it kind of disturbs our whole—

MK

Serenity.
[Jek Mui laughs]

Jek Mui

So I guess it's the mindset or the attitude towards control. I think it takes time and practice to be able to see things in a very neutral way, to actually let go, because there are things you can control, and there are things you really can't control. It's about recognizing it, what you can or can't influence. So things that you can do, you go and do. If you have no control and you can't do anything, you can try—it's not that you can't—but you also have to be aware of the impact and consequences if you were to try. In that sense, it's seeing it with a bit more neutrality. But to be very honest, this neutrality doesn't come on day one when you land the job. At the start, you will be thinking, wah, how can this be like that? But it takes time to build that resilience and reflect on why things are like this. And when we ask why, we're not really asking or looking for an answer. It's more of just okay, so things are like this. But . . .

MK

What do I do?

Jek Mui

Yeah. What can I do? Is there something I can do? No? Okay, then how? It's also preparing yourself that if you can't do anything, then you just have to wait. Flow with it. One of the metaphors that I like to share with my colleagues is that it's like a river. I think when we look at the river, it looks still, but it's actually flowing all the time. And I use this metaphor because it's like change. It's always there, it's just how observant you are. Are you seeing that the water is actually flowing?

And I think it's up to you whether you want to be the person to stand at the bank to look at the river flow, or have the faith and courage to jump in and flow with the river to wherever it takes you. To be honest, there's a lot of fear. The joke that I crack with them is that you don't know whether this river, like in some cartoons, flows into a waterfall. You don't know if you will free fall down the waterfall, or whether you will flow into the ocean peacefully. So you don't know where it takes you. There's the excitement, and at the same time, there's a lot of fear around what's going to happen because of the uncertainty. It's about how you manage and navigate this uncertainty because nothing is certain in life. If you think that this is fixed, then when it's changed, definitely you—

MK

You're going to react!

Jek Mui

Because you have no control over it! So if you have a mindset that things will—

MK

Must be like this, or must be like that.

Jek Mui

Things will not last forever even though they are there for a long time.

MK

That is some real wisdom.

Jek Mui

So then what can you do? You can use a different framework to look at change, because change is the only thing that is constant. So how do you work with that? I guess it's always these few words that remind me that, well, we all suffer. We all struggle in our lives. We're all humans. We all have a voice, and we all—

MK

We're all fighting different battles in our lives.

Jek Mui

Correct. I could be having a chronic condition that nobody knows about and I'm struggling inside in silence. When you look at me, you may think oh, she's good, she's fine, she's healthy, but I'm not. So we have all these challenges, whether small or big. Whether it's already diagnosed clinically, or not it doesn't matter. I think in life we all go through that and what's helpful for us to know is that we all struggle, and we're not alone. Even though it sounds a bit lonely!

[Jek Mui laughs]

But we're not alone, actually. And I think that's the common humanity that we actually talk about . . . There could be someone else like me out there in the community. It's just that I haven't got the chance to know them. So it's common humanity, and I think what we can then offer to ourselves is kindness. What do I need? It's about being mindful and having self-compassion. When I reflect on the tools and skills I've learned along the way, I think mindfulness and self-compassion are very helpful.

So of course, at this point, people will ask, there's sympathy, empathy, there's compassion. So what's the difference? And compassion is the action to alleviate the person from suffering.

THE IMPORTANCE OF PERSON-CENTRED CARE

MK

Got it. The next question I have is, would you say dementia is a mental illness?

[Jek Mui laughs]

MK

It's one of the hardest questions, isn't it?

[Jek Mui laughs]

Jek Mui

It is common that when people think about dementia, they associate it to mental illness due to the effects it has on the brain. There are distinctions that should be made between dementia and mental illness to properly diagnose the individual. While dementia does affect mental health, it is not a mental illness. It is a disorder of the brain, a decline in mental ability which affects memory, thinking, problem-solving, concentration, and perception.

For people living with dementia, they may experience low moods because they're constantly wondering where am I? Why am I being told to do things? Why is this person being very harsh towards me? They may experience low moods, and after a prolonged period, it could lead to depression. The most common question is, is this depression, or is this dementia? For people living with dementia, they may experience depression at some point in life because of the many transitions they go through, such as the losses in their life in terms of identity, their own health, or the people around them as they age. If you were to really put it under a mental illness, based on my understanding, it would be things like schizophrenia, personality disorder, anxiety, or depression. So to me, I see it as a brain disease.

MK

Got it. More of a physical brain disease that leads to mental health symptoms subsequently?

Jek Mui

May or may not. Each individual is different, because it depends on the support systems around them.

MK

Yeah, the support systems around them. Got it. How important are these support systems in the community?

Jek Mui

I think when we talk about support systems, there are two. One is the internal, from within the person themselves, and then there's the external.

So when you talk about the community, it's the people around them. In the community, there are daycare services, home care services, or palliative care, depending on the stage they're in. There are befriending services, there are nurses, community nurses who go to the homes as well, rehabilitation, and different therapies. The different roles of the partners serve different functions for them. If the persons require physio to maintain their muscles, then they would need a physiotherapist. So again, it's very individualized, based on the needs of the person. It's important, and that's why part of the services we offer here includes providing support groups for fellow caregivers to come together to talk about their struggles. In a two-hour session, we spend one hour on dementia-related information, and the other hour for them to share their experiences. We also have interest groups as well because as caregivers, sometimes they may have given up their own hopes and dreams in order to care for the person that they love. They may want to develop a new interest, but are unable to find the time or the space to actually do that. So some of the classes we have are things like guitar strumming, knitting and crochet classes. I think we are starting a zentangle class too. Having interest groups actually help caregivers to also remain socially connected.

When we talk about inner resources, it's the buoyancy that they have, the resilience, their coping mechanisms. I think

for us, it's about how we can continue to support the person. In dementia care, the late professor Tom Kitwood once said that one of the key things is person-centred care. How do you maintain this personhood for this person, to continue supporting what the person actually likes? If the person likes to go to the library, how can we facilitate this activity for this person? It's about being inclusive, asking what the person actually wants and not saying *now it's time for dinner, go!*
[Jek Mui laughs]

But when do we get that? Probably when we were a child. But this person has a life, maybe about fifty years old, sixty or eighty, and you're saying, eat your dinner now. So the way you communicate, the tone of your voice, is also very important. Most people would say it's a role reversal, but it's also a mindset. If you have that role reversal idea, it's like now I become a parent to my parents. Then the way that you communicate may be different. I'm not saying that it's wrong, I'm saying that there may be a different way to communicate, and it takes skills, practice and willingness to change, because can you imagine; I'm rushing for time, I prepare the meal, and I tell them just eat! Why can't you just eat? So again, it's patience. Being able to go with the person's pace because the person's thinking ability has slowed down.

GIVING BACK TO THE CAREGIVERS

MK

Got it. A lot of caregivers devote a lot of energy into caring for people living with dementia and end up getting so burnt out or exhausted that they don't even have the energy left for themselves. What do you think is causing that, and how do you think it has improved over the last few years?
[silence]

Jek Mui

I think first and foremost, it is the awareness and understanding of what is stressful for the person. So again, it's very individualized because we have different threshold levels. What's stressful for you, I think for me okay lah. So it's understanding yourself and your limits. And understanding what it's like when you're not coping well. What would be some physical signs? Is it tiredness, or the lack of energy? Is it mental? Is it emotional? Do you flare up more? So a question to ask is, how would you know that you are stressed? How would you know that you're not able to cope? So first it's recognizing that. And it's also the awareness of the telltale signs of stress and burnout. In caregiving, we talk about the oxygen mask as a metaphor.

MK

Tell me more.
[Jek Mui laughs]

Jek Mui

How could you not have heard of it?

MK

No, this is the first time I'm hearing it!

Jek Mui

Huh! Seriously?

MK

Yeah!

Jek Mui

So in airplanes, if there is a sudden drop in cabin pressure and the oxygen mask drops, the instruction given is to always wear your own mask before helping others put it on. Imagine helping others before you put on your own mask. You'd be the one running out of oxygen! If you run out of oxygen first, you can't help others! Taking care of yourself is your own responsibility before you can take care of others. Of course, I just want to add that as caregivers, because of the relationship that they have with the care recipients, they devote their love, their time, their undivided attention, which I think is really nice and lovely to have. But I think it's also about knowing that you do have your own needs and you do need to address your own needs.

MK

What do you think, from an organizational or even a societal point of view, can we do to ensure that the caregivers are taken care of?

Jek Mui

I think there are two groups that you're talking about. One is the family caregivers, including helpers, because of the dynamics and demographics right now. The other group is the professional caregivers who are paid. For family caregivers of persons living with dementia, it's not that it's not possible, but it's rare to get a smile from them, a thanks, or even a hug, or a handshake.
[Jek Mui laughs]

The reciprocity from care recipients, in the form of expressing their love and gratitude to their caregivers can be rather lacking. I think what caregivers would like to have is to just be appreciated.

MK

That sounds more like an individual thing, but what about collective? What are some things that can be implemented? One of the things that I found out after talking to a few caregivers is that caregivers are often underpaid.
[Jek Mui hmm-ing]

Jek Mui

. . . Or no pay lah.
[Jek Mui laughs]

MK

Is that a sweeping statement?

Jek Mui

I think it depends on the context. If we talk about family caregivers, I don't think underpaid seems to be the right word. Because first and foremost, they're not paid most of the time.

MK

Yup.

Jek Mui

Yeah. How you become a caregiver could be a result of you just happening to be the youngest, happening to be earning the lowest income, or happening to have a close relationship with mum and that's why you're the caregiver.

MK

I see . . .

Jek Mui

So when they do give up their job, economically, it's their impact to society, to the nation. Even though they earn a low income, it's also an impact. And what most families do is that they will contribute towards the care of their mother. But if you are the caregiver, you are kind of on your own. Some families do give allowance to the caregiver, but not a lot. And I think that's one of the factors that caregivers also struggle with; I give up my job, I look after my mother, but I don't get a word of thanks, and here she is asking for my brother who doesn't visit.

[Jek Mui laughs]

Brother gives money, but brother doesn't do it. I'm doing the hard work, but she's always yelling for him. I'm cleaning her, I'm doing everything! So when I put it in terms of appreciation and recognition, due to the care recipient's cognitive ability, they may not express themselves well, and even the family is not appreciative of what they're doing. If, for example, mum had a fall, then you get questions like why did you let that happen?

I think, for a start, it is to learn how we can settle in and transition into someone who is a caregiver. Of course, over the years, there have been discussions about how we can recognize caregivers on a national level. There are caregivers awards that you can nominate people for. There's also talk about whether there could be monetary rewards to caregivers, so that has been in discussion.

MK

Got it.

Jek Mui

And I think if you talk about nurses, social workers, and people in the helping professions . . . Because we are in the profession, over the years, there's income adjustment lah. But you know again, it's a question of how much you think you should be paid versus how much is paid to you. So, no matter how much you pay me, if my attitude is still that I need more, it will never be enough.

MK

It's never enough.

Jek Mui

Yes, yes. There has been adjustment. It's up to the individual whether that adjustment is good enough, or not good enough.

CONNECTION IS JOY

MK

Got it. My last question to you would be this: what does connection mean to you?
[silence]

Jek Mui

Joy?
[Jek Mui laughs]
In a simple way, I love the word connection, or connect. It brings people together, that's why I use joy. Because in dementia, I think one of the earlier programmes that I facilitated, I called it 'Connecting the Dots'. It's also a game that we always used to play when we were young. When you see the dots, you cannot form the image, but when you actually follow and you connect it, you can actually see the big picture. Mm. That's all!

MK

What does human connection mean to you?

Jek Mui

It's a very important element, human connection. The basic need to form, grow, and sustain relationships and belong to a group, team or family, is universal. We are social creatures. We all need real connection, dependable emotional support, and a feeling of belonging, whoever we are, wherever we are. Connections nourish us and our connections to others gives so much meaning to our lives. Knowing that you're not alone in this path and there's always someone with you.

MK

And it's never too late to ask for help.

Jek Mui

Yes!

CHAPTER THIRTEEN

Everything Goes Back to Choice

Marion Neubronner, Psychologist and Leadership Development Coach

Marion talks about the individual choices we make that create the circumstances and environment we live in. In order to break free from them, we need to recognize that we have a part to play in creating our circumstances, and the choices we knowingly or unknowingly make. Marion shares the importance of having a personal responsibility to own our lives and the choice we make to change it for the better.

TEACHING AND INSPIRING OTHERS

MK

What made you decide to walk on the path that you've walked so far?

Marion

My passion is education. I believe that when people are educated, they can understand an issue or learn how to learn about issues. They then can help themselves and they can help others. I believe education can change the world, and my part in it is to educate as many people as possible in things that will help them. I do a lot of personal development, resilience, mental health, mindfulness, nutrition, longevity. Just to optimize people lah, I think that's a better way of looking at it. Optimize yourself so that you can do more things for yourself and others.

Another gift I have is that apparently, I'm a good writer. And this is what people have told me. It started when I was in the US, and I would write home to tell my friends and family about what I'm doing and my experiences. People often said they felt they were there with me. Another example was when I wrote about how I did not say I love you to my father when he was dying because he was an alcoholic and I was very frustrated with him most of my life. I took care of him as he was dying, but I never said I love you at the end because I didn't feel like it. And then I wrote this whole piece. A lot of people commented, and one person said that he actually called his father to say I love you because of my post, so like that lah. Writing and processing emotions is one of the things I do.

I've conducted some online courses as well. Many people come to me to learn counselling skills because I was teaching people to be either counsellors, coaches, or people who were interested in learning psychology. Those who are more self-aware are aware that they have their own challenges, and that while they're learning all these counselling skills, they didn't really apply these skills to themselves.

But the moment they started applying it to themselves, they saw things they realized they were not looking at, or things they were avoiding. And if people like yourself, Ming Kwang, or anyone in the community says that they need my psychological understanding on something, I do volunteer to help, or provide educational understanding.

THE FLIPSIDE OF STIGMA: EVERY ACTION OR INACTION IS STILL A CHOICE WE MAKE

MK

Let's look into the whole subject of mental health. What are the stigmas that you've observed, and what are the differences in stigmas here compared to other countries?

Marion

Stigma is something that prevents you from seeking help. And it's quite strong, meaning the whole society is against it. Think of diseases like HIV. That's stigma. But the examples I have are not stigma. They are choices. And when you choose one identity over another identity so strongly, you feel that you cannot cheat or remove that first identity.

Regrettably, I deal with a lot of people who have been cheated or abused by bullies, or mostly spouses who are men. Of course, it also could be the other way. One example is regarding a very well-achieved Filipino woman who had a very good family background, and married a very successful Filipino man who's quite well known too, but it was not a healthy husband-wife relationship and not a healthy family relationship. When she came to me, she wanted to learn a certain skill. So she met me through the coaching course, but years later, she called me and told me her entire story of how her husband was basically verbally abusive and controlling. And one of her sons was also very exploitative, and they were using her for money and depending on her for things. This woman is not young, not uneducated, but she had chosen for too many years the path of a wife and mother in a manner that hid from people the fact that her household was in a mess, that she was in pain and unhappy. So she came to Singapore. Already, getting on the plane by herself was difficult for her, and this is not the first woman I've heard of, of a certain age range, who cannot travel by themselves. So in such instances, I cannot call it stigma. I would say that they have the ability, but they're afraid.

MK

They chose.

Marion

They chose to be under someone who directed and managed their lives for them. So perhaps you'll ask me, why didn't she reach out earlier? If you believe that you are part of a group that functions this way, then they chose to be unhappy to keep the stability of the identity of wife, mother, achieved person in society, and what other names they have in society lah. I never blame the other person. It's never a black and white situation, she must have done something that caused him to be like that as well. But the point is, there's no stigma there, it was literally choices that may have helped her initially, but did not help her later on. Then to keep that first choice even though you're unhappy or unwell because of it, is a choice! So I wouldn't call it stigma. We don't label it stigma, a choice is a choice, right?

MK

A choice is still a choice. Not choosing is also a choice.

Marion

Any place where there's a dominant person and you choose to keep living in that situation, be it at the workplace or at home, and you do not come out and say how unhappy you are, is a choice that you make.

We are born happy. When we're unhappy for natural reasons like there's not enough something, that's a disappointment. And then when we're unhappy for a long time, in order to pretend that we're happy, we do stupid things like drink a lot, which a lot of people I know do.

MK

It's called suffering.

Marion

Every show you watch, Korean or American shows, whenever they're sad, alcohol is brought out. We need alcohol to be able to speak freely. And there are other trends, not just alcohol. Eat and forget. Drink and forget. Shop and forget. Any kind of -holic. Workaholic, shopaholic. Are you using these things to make you happy? If you don't really know why you do something, or you're just doing it because it's fun, can lah. But if you become overweight, or you get sick, or you wake up and forget your days, then no lah, you're not just enjoying yourself. You're a -holic. Then your happiness is not satisfying you. And it's an expectation for when you cannot accept that it's like that. You cannot accept the situation as it is and your state of mind is unhappiness.

MK

Again, it's a choice.

Marion

Definitely a choice. See, so the choice of a certain commitment regardless of how it's affecting you is very powerful. And mental health is health. How do you know you're healthy? You wake up, you are driven by something you want to do, you have ups and downs, but mostly, there are more ups than downs. Or you're at peace, and you don't resent the people in your lives or yourself. I resented my father for a long time, so I wouldn't say I was mentally healthy. I was definitely in a position of being bullied and victimized, but slowly as I grew older, I had more resources, and I became more empowered to care for myself despite the fact that my father was an alcoholic with a very bad temper.

You choose the people in your life. My father had problems with alcohol and was abusive. Didn't hit us. Threatened to, but didn't hit me at least. But he was also my loving father. He also loved me to bits. He also provided for me materially. So it comes with two forces. But the example I gave you about the women are not about two forces, they're about—

MK

One force.

Marion

Yes, and they chose. So with my father . . . Look, I distanced myself. I had my own room. I spoke less to him, but that was a choice, to stay in the same house and do that. And also knowing he was both dark and light at the same time. And I also had my mum in the house, so my choice was to stay there for my mum, and for my dad, there was no resolution or breakthrough. It just was. You've got to choose one of your burdens in life, right? But your burden does not have to be this master and slave driver dynamic which some of these examples are more clearly about.

I've no resentment now, but a lot of forgiveness over the years for myself and him lah. So the best way I forgave him was to realize that he was not an alcoholic. He was a victim of alcoholism. He was alcoholic as a sickness. So some of the choices he made were like how a sick person would make those choices, and he became like that because his own family was messed up and he felt that that was his way to keep himself happy. To drink, smoke, gamble, say terrible things about people. But you see, the fact that I can see that he was trying not to be like that, that I can choose my own path, says that he gave me enough of a chance to be aware.

ADDICTIONS REVEAL OUR RELATIONSHIPS WITH OURSELVES, OTHERS, AND THE WORLD

MK

Okay, let's look into the addiction side, since that came up. Alcoholism, even violence, is part of it. What is the underlying factor that causes a person to be addicted to something?

Marion

That this behaviour for them is normal. Think about alcohol and smoking. In all studies, if you smoke underage, it's not because it's age. It's because your body gets it too early and it thinks it's normal, it thinks it's nutrition. Then you get addicted because you feel you want it again and again. And when you're younger, your body cannot process smoking, so the child is again taking in things that are way before their time. So, when you as a parent try to delay anything, less smoking, less drinking, less alcohol, less sex, less everything right, you actually give them a point where they're more conscious of choosing. If I want to drink alcohol, I can buy it when I know I can handle it, when I'm eighteen or so. If I want to be in a relationship with someone, I build a relationship where there's safety. So addiction, the earlier you start, the worse lah. Simple as that. And it's normally like that because the child or young person is put in a place where it's considered normal, easy to access—even good to access—there is the danger. When they become adults in any form, they are quicker to drink, smoke, anything else, chocoholic or shopaholic. Shopping for clothes is not an issue of the clothes what, it's an issue of when I wear those clothes, I feel good, like my identity is different.

Addiction is when it crosses the mark of balance to overdoing it. How would we know that? You have to try yourself and find the difference between an empowered choice and an unconscious choice driven by an internal need to fill up something within through an external act.

MK

If you keep creating the same thing again and again, something internally is not right, and you're trying to use that to fill up or mask something that's really inside.

Marion

Correct, correct. It's an internal discussion. I can give you my -holism. I thought about it. I'm a recovered workaholic. So what happens in Singapore is that a lot of us use work as a way of filling up the emptiness. And also to not go home! It's been shown again, many children rather stay at school than go home because their home is messed up. So for me with the alcoholic father then, I'd rather stay in school. But when I was working, I was so devoted to my work, my safe space, my air-conditioner. That's what we are doing now, which is a good thing for the economy, but it's bad when you don't realize that you are giving up your time and energy to remove the excessive energy of the displeasure or unhappiness in your life.

But sports people don't need to. They can run, but they also have a -holism, which is too much sports, because it gives them so much pleasure until they go overboard. So any -ism is not about the manner, it is about which one you choose. It just so happens that some of them like sports and workaholism are to your benefit, somewhat. But it doesn't mean that it's not an -ism. So yeah, I'm a recovering workaholic, a very happy workaholic. I get a lot done, get a lot of good things in my life from it, but that doesn't mean it was good because there was part of my life that I ignored or pretended didn't exist by using work to distract myself.

MK

So addiction is also about connecting with ourselves and understanding that we're trying to fill up something. It tells us about our relationship with ourselves. And our relationship with ourselves also reflects our relationships with other people, and also our relationship with the world. It still goes back to who am I?

Marion

So, for example, I am conflict-avoidant. I don't like to go near conflict. How did I become like this? It's so obvious! When you're a child and your father is an alcoholic person with a bad temper like mine, your mum might have taught you to be very quiet and hide your whole life. That's what happened. So whenever my father came home, I became quieter. I hid in the room with my book. That's how I kept safe. Obviously, when I went out into the real world, the same, right? If there's a large person making noise, I hide in one corner and read a book even though I'm an adult.

MK

This behaviour continues to follow us into adulthood as though it is normal.

Marion

And as though the past is in the present. And you feel that it's because of the hormones. It is not true. So when I meet someone outside, I don't like excessive excitement in the environment.

MK

Anything that pushes you out of—

Marion

Correct, out of my safe quiet space. That goes back to the same challenge, isn't it? That is why I say you must understand that it's not addiction, but being so used to that feeling of comfort that I would rather avoid conflict than engage. I have to teach myself to engage more.

I will share a story. Once, at an international event, a male Indian speaker said something, and a woman stood up and questioned that man about something he said, or the way he said it, and he just said no, that's not true. At the moment, I didn't say anything. And I sat with it and realized I wanted to say something, but I didn't. It was a 200-participant entrepreneur conference. The man wasn't mean, and the woman wasn't either. It's just that she said a point, and he didn't hear it. After a few days, I actually went to the woman and told her that I should have said something because I agreed with you, but I didn't, and I'm sorry I didn't support your view, and she said she understood.

But I also went to the guy and said to him, when you said that to her, I didn't speak out, but I agreed with her. It's not as tough as you make it sound, and he said ah yes, you're right, and he accepted it. So I reconciled it in my own way, but I didn't do it at that point because I was overwhelmed by my own story to run away from conflict and refrain from getting involved so that I wouldn't get hurt. That's not the person I am now. Now I'm better lah. That was ten years ago.

MK

So that was when you were trying to correct something in your default mode, and you decided to do something you have never done. That is your way and approach to reconcile.

Marion

I had to because I felt sick. There was this natural instinct to know that something wasn't right.

But other people would normally turn to addiction, or hiding, or drinking, or sleeping, or talking it out of their system.

MK

Got it. And what did you gain out of doing something that's different?

Marion

I respect myself more. My integrity is high. I say this not to blow my own trumpet. I say this out of self-awareness.

It's also because when I run my own business, it's very simple. I want or don't want, it's up to me. I blame myself all the time, right? So if I'm going to give my word, I will do just that. Sometimes now, when I see something I don't want, I walk away, and I know I can support myself some other way or make money somewhere else or find another way.

But to be very fair, anyone who's burdened or responsible for a family, or is working in a bigger corporate entity or government, they play with a lot of grey areas. And the world is grey! Grey is a challenging space to be in. That's why I say everything is in a continuum. But I can live with it.

UNDERSTANDING WHY WE RESIST CHANGE SPARKS EVOLUTION

MK

So how can individuals raise their level of awareness so that they can really see what's going on around them?

Marion

Most people end up being more self-aware during crises or transitions, and that's why you always say oh they'll grow up when they reach puberty or university. Or when they get their first job, they'll wake up. But that's a rite of passage type of thing. In cultures, there are rites of passage. By default, society has created it in such a way that supposedly, because of the functions and roles you play, when you become a father, you will stop smoking. When you go to university, you'll study harder, because you're going after a career. So the word 'individuals' needs to be more defined because of two things: how much responsibility you hold, and how much impact that responsibility has.

So if you ask how we can help people have more self-awareness . . . Really, the bigger the project they undertake, the more self-awareness they will gain, because the feedback mechanisms are larger. If I'm the mother of a child, I'll receive feedback from my child, my husband, and my in-laws. So there's a lot of feedback. In fact, someone once said that the greatest growth feedback is when you get married or start your own business, because both require huge and rigorous commitment and provide immense feedback loops. So the first thing I'll say to you is not to read a book to become more self-aware. It's to read a book for context. For parents, you read a parenting book. For teachers, you read an educational book. So there's the feedback loop. So the answer is, know what you want to do, and as you grow into being the best you can do for the role or project, self-awareness can develop!

MK

Got it. I totally agree, because I myself walked through the journey too. The larger the project, the higher the scale, the more you have to open your eyes up, and open your awareness up so that everything is taken care of. Otherwise, everything can go south.

Marion

Yeah, that's why I like peak performers, because they choose bigger things to run after. And I'm sorry to say, I have very few Singaporean friends who are peak performers because all the average Singaporean typically does is really just eat, work, sleep, family. But that's the normal grind, and it's not bad, but when something challenging happens, usually they cannot cope.

MK

Correct. When a crisis happens, it crashes their whole psyche. Alright, so my thing is this. I totally agree with what you said. Let's say for people who are not in touch with the bigger projects they can take, how can they build their self-awareness?

Marion

Normally we only solve the things in front of us. So let's say I've been molested. I solve that by teaching girls what to watch out for. I take police action. I write a whitepaper. It's up to me. Do I want to take it to a larger scale, or do I just solve what's in front of me and ignore the rest? If you live in India now, no choice, right? You will have to take this issue on. So it's not an issue of whether people don't have a mission. Everyone has a choice for a mission. It's just whether you take it to a larger scale or not. And for those who do not have any challenges to solve, who seem to be lucky enough to live with very few challenges, they should look around and see whose challenges they are responsible for helping to solve.

I mean, if you think of life force as an energy that's given to you, and you have a certain amount of life force a day, you take up the mission according to how much you want to fulfil. So it's literally a choice. I think maybe I will rephrase your question for you because the context is crucial to this discussion. Let's start with these premises.

Number one. Why do people give themselves up fully or unconditionally? Why do they give their lives away? Firefighters, nurses, or anything that may be more challenging. Most of the time, when you ask them, they don't feel that they have a choice. That's their job, that's their mission, that is their thing. That's their journey of self-awareness. So my thing is I'm a teacher. I still like teaching, and I write quite well, so that has become my thing. So when I talk about my father's alcoholism, I don't educate alcoholics. I don't go to prisons and help. I write, that's what I do. That's my thing, my contribution, and my mission. And the more I write, the more I deepen that, the more self-aware I become from the feedback I get.

But if you do put someone in a place they totally don't want to be, that means it's not their mission. But they will also learn. They will just learn how to avoid it, avoid the pain and suffering. For example, in the movie *Shawshank Redemption*, an innocent man ends up in prison, and he cannot be the nice person there. He has to act according to the system in order to get out. So if a young teenage girl ends up accidentally having a child before her time, then she grows up fast, but she grows in a way that wasn't aligned to her choice—or even society's choice—of growing. She is growing in a way that's necessary for her at the moment.

MK

So for people who are being placed in those circumstances, they will avoid it?

Marion

You keep saying as if they're being placed. No one's placed! You choose all your choices.

MK

Correct, they choose. But you know when they choose that position, they don't necessarily uphold the responsibility and ownership of that position. Which means that they may not even own the choice they make. They may start avoiding and evading.

Marion

Normally, yes. So for example, you cannot blame a teenage boy and girl when they accidentally have a child because they lost themselves in the throes of love, or whatever. That one time becomes a really big thing unless they abort. That one time was such a small responsibility, like putting on a condom, but when it escalates into such a big thing, most people will not claim it. They will ask why is life so difficult? Why life so bad? Not my fault. But this big thing came from your small responsibility. If you claim the big thing, you grow from the experience. You got no choice but to grow what, because it's a huge life change. From teenager to parent.

So the answer is we choose everything. Sometimes we cannot choose so wisely because we're not fully capable of understanding what we're doing. And luck of the draw, something happens. Then, as you said, if we accept it totally, we can grow from it. But if we keep avoiding it, the same lesson is always there. It's just that we're avoiding it, and we're helpless. The victim.

MK

You will find reasons to put blame on.

Marion

You will find any way to avoid it lah. But avoiding has its pleasures and enjoyment and ownership.

MK

Yeah, but that goes against the person's development, growth, and evolution as well.

Marion

I think the resistance to change is evolution. I think understanding why we resist change is evolution.

LEARNT HELPLESSNESS: THERE IS ALWAYS A WAY OUT

MK

What do you think communities and individuals can do as an intervention to reduce stigmas around mental health?

Marion

There's too much learnt helplessness. Learnt helplessness, in this case in Singapore, would be that young people don't think they have options. They think they have to live in a very expensive country, when they could actually be working in another part of the world that's more affordable and more likely to need their youths and talents. You have the perception that you cannot change your circumstance, so you accept the circumstance as it is. In our culture, there is a lot of learnt helplessness. I'll give you an example. I have friends who lived in China who are not Chinese. They said that when they lived in China at that time, especially when the internet was very slow and they had to call the internet technician, the internet technician just said it's China, right? It's China. Then my international friends said, after living there for a while, even the local young Chinese people would say it's f**king China. So you get used to not expecting something that the circumstances cannot give you, and there's passive aggression there. So learnt helplessness, or passive aggression, happens because you accept this box that you're living in. But the first thing is, philosophically, there's no box. Really, you can always find your way out. Just redefine the situation. Take ownership, do not be a victim.

MK

You're the one who created the box in the first place, and you have the power to walk out from it, that's what you're saying. But people don't necessarily have the awareness to recognize that.

Marion

What the community can do is learn to understand that they cannot let anyone or any child think there is no way out. There is always a way out.

MK

There is always a way out.

If you had a message to the public around mental health, emotional wellness, and also suicide prevention, what would it be? [silence, Marion thinking]

Marion

Grieve if you are sad, but give it just one more day before you do anything else. Grieve and tahan one more day. Grieve and cry one more day, that's what I say. I used to teach in an all-boys school, and we had some senior boys commit suicide which, of course, impacted the junior boys. So I remember telling them, no matter what, before you do the stupid thing, you call me. And then I made them promise to call me before they do anything to themselves, because I can't help you if you don't. But the more important thing is that you know you'll hurt me if you do that, and I'm not trying to guilt trip you. It's not just me who will be hurt, but many people as well. So before you do anything, you better call me. So at that moment of choice, breathe, and just try to give it more time and space, and usually something will sort itself out. It will usually get better, not worse. It just is challenging lah. And it's challenging for so long that people get tired, that's the real answer.

CHAPTER FOURTEEN

Take Time Off to Honour Yourself

By Carrie Tan, Member of Parliament, Chairperson of Nee Soon South (Nee Soon GRC)

Mental health came to the forefront of Ms Tan's life when a close family member grappled with a mental health condition. As she reflects on what her family member had to go through, as well as her own struggles during her twenties, she stresses the importance of setting aside time to be with yourself and honour yourself.

VERBALISING YOUR CHALLENGES

MK

Tell me more about your work!
[Carrie laughs]

Carrie

I'm a politician, I'm a community builder, and I think I can call myself a serial social entrepreneur because I started my second non-profit. There are so many dimensions to my work. As an MP[11], I've represented my constituents in Parliament, represented Singaporeans in Parliament on issues they care about, that I care about. On a municipal level, I am a channel for residents to sound out problems they encounter in their day-to-day municipal experience, in their living environment, whether things are working well, whether amenities are working well, etc. I am often a mediator of different relationships within the community, whether it's person to person, organization to organization, or groups to groups. I'm also facilitating initiatives that provide some kind of value add to residents' lives. For example, facilitating initiatives that centre around mental health awareness, around support for caregivers. So these are various things that I do. I don't think that properly covers 100 per cent of what I do but, in a nutshell, it's all these things.

MK

Got it. I think over the last few years, you have been doing a lot of work advocating for mental health, and that includes you sharing your own personal journey too.

---

[11] MP: Member of Parliament

Carrie

Well, I didn't really plan it that way. Most of my work has been around uplifting the underprivileged, starting from mothers, women, and now with the new non-profit, men as well.

But the mental health piece came about much more recently because of a close family member and the fact that we grappled with caring for someone with a mental health condition. That personal experience of having to manage that and seeing the realities of what someone who is inflicted with a mental health condition has to go through, and the implications on their jobs, on their relationships within the family, all these things start to present themselves very starkly to me while I'm in the thick of it. In fact, it was very trying for myself on my own mental health when there was a period of time, and this was before politics right, when I was juggling multiple roles in my job at Daughters of Tomorrow and pursuing my Master's education, which was quite a lot of things. I was also in the process of potentially entering politics at that time, so there was a lot of stuff happening on my plate, and having to deal with a loved one's relapse in a mental health condition was quite simply overwhelming. And yet because in a small family, I had to be there for my parents while they are also navigating this and managing this you know. It felt like you have to be there for everyone. It takes a huge toll when you find yourself at that point in time having to be there for everyone.

MK

And how does that impact or affect your own mental health journey?

Carrie

Hmm. I think it was tough and I mean thankfully, I also had other loved ones like my partner who was there, who was very good at holding space for me to let out my emotions and my frustrations without judgement. And I think that was very precious and it helped a lot. In fact, I cannot imagine what it's like if anyone, when faced with circumstances like that, when there's just so much on your shoulders, does not have someone they can talk to who doesn't judge any of their feelings. I can't imagine what then would be the consequence of anyone having to go through that alone. But I guess the good thing about me is that I am quite vocal. And I'm quite open. I tend not to hide what I'm going through, so it's easy for me to verbalize my challenges to people, to my support system, and because I reached out, there was also ample support for me. I think what others may experience is they may not feel so at ease in reaching out to people around them and hence, they may not have as many opportunities for people to come give them support. I think that would be one of the key challenges that anyone, when facing an overburdened load, may find challenging.

CREATING AN INCLUSIVE COMMUNITY

MK

Got it. What are some of these stigmas that you observed as you are on the ground and also in your own personal mental health journey? Stigmas around mental health.

Carrie Tan

Well, for example, when I go on my house visits, couple of times I've come across residents who open their door just a little bit and are very cursory. They're friendly, but what I've observed is that family members tend to want to hide away their family members who may have a mental health condition. I can sense that they're ashamed or embarrassed about their family members having an affliction.

It was quite heartbreaking because I've seen how, when I provide a reassuring word or two to say hey don't hide your daughter or don't hide your who and who, or it's okay, this is quite common and I think he or she would like to say hi and I would like to say hi to him or her, I don't know what that leaves them with.

But definitely for the person who was trying to reach out, I can sense the joy when they are seen, when they are acknowledged by a stranger who has come forward. So I guess I would just keep doing that more when I come across it.

MK

Was that a specific incident?

Carrie Tan

Yeah that was a specific incident. It was an elderly auntie and her adult daughter behind the door. I don't know what her condition is, but I saw the desire of her daughter to want to reach out and say hi and just you know, have a friendly chat.

MK

What happened after that?

Carrie Tan

What happened after that is I decided that we needed to set up some mental health initiatives in Nee Soon South so that we can create an environment where people feel less ashamed or less embarrassed about people around them having mental health conditions, and to create a more embracing culture where it's okay if you're different, or it's okay if you're struggling with something. And you may not appear very normal in public, but it's okay to be yourself and as a neighbourhood, as a community, we have people here in the community who understand what it's like and can relate to you so that you can take part in everyday activities without having to fear that people are looking at you strangely.

MK

Well, brainstorm a little bit with me. I'm not sure whether it makes sense or not, but what do you think is really holding people back from seeking help? For example, using the story that you just shared as a case, perhaps people hold themselves back because there was undisclosed shame due to judgements. What do you think?

Carrie Tan

Yeah. Well maybe I can share another story. It's about a very close friend of mine who lost her father a few years ago. Obviously, it was a very very difficult time for her because she was very close to her dad who wasn't that old at that time. I would say he passed quite prematurely for his age and my friend was really struggling through the grieving process. She works in a tech company where on top of being the minority of females in the company and all the layers of perceptions or things she has to navigate as a female, she also had to struggle with how the grief would overwhelm her even at work. She would cry and she would beat herself up over it like why can't I pull myself together? People lose their loved ones and I don't see people crying in the office and she had a judgement towards herself as being somehow not strong enough, not being able to get it together.

I think sometimes it could be the individual's expectations of how we should just get it together and move on that prevents people from reaching out, that it's a sign of weakness and somehow the notion that being weak is bad. I mean if you really go down to it, the notion that being weak is bad or being weak is lesser could fundamentally be the thing that prevents people from reaching out because they don't want to be seen as being weak.

THE COMPLEXITIES OF GROWING UP: FINDING YOUR VOICE

MK

And how do you think as a society, people are generally dealing with that? I mean these days, there's a lot more awareness of mental health. People are talking more about mental health, people are more expressive when it comes to their feelings all that, but something is still missing.

Carrie Tan

I think definitely what I've encountered is that there's a difficulty amongst different generations of people in empathizing with those who struggle with mental health. For example, one of it is that the younger generation seems to be presenting with more mental health struggles and people from the older generation will use terms like strawberry generation lah, why so fragile lah, and all that. And I mean that's not helpful for sure, but I have to say sometimes I also, when pushed to frustration about how come I can't seem to be able to reach out to someone, or someone isn't able to lift themselves out of a tough situation, I find myself veering towards making or having a judgemental thought like that too. I'm not perfect in this either.

MK

How does knowing who you are as a person link to mental health and emotional wellness?

Carrie Tan

Well, I think just based on my own personal journey, I'm so thankful to now be heading into my thirty-ninth year. If you ask me like oh youth is great, right? I would never want to go back to my twenties to be honest, because I think in my twenties there was a lot of confusion. People are telling you different things about what you should be, and it was a whole decade, a whole era, maybe it started from thirteen, fourteen, fifteen years old, just trying to understand who you are, how you fit in, what's the right thing to do, what's the not right thing to do, competing pressures. And it's confusing because you have a voice in yourself at that age, but that voice is not very pronounced. And perhaps as I was growing up, that voice was not very encouraged to come out and assert itself so that little voice was kind of suppressed suppressed suppressed. And the whole cacophony of voices of society was coming at you and okay, who do you listen to?

And I think it was after I went through an episode of domestic violence, it catalysed a period of deep introspection and reflection that lasted several years, and I was able to find my own voice. And that became the fundamental anchor for myself and in a way, an anchor for my sanity, for my mental health amidst everything else that was going on around me, all the voices that you hear from society. So I think having this strong voice inside yourself to anchor who you are, what you believe in, what you stand for, was tremendously critical for me to then be able to proceed on in my various roles in life with much more ease. I mean it doesn't mean that the challenges disappear but with the anchor, you're able to navigate and overcome challenges without breaking apart.

SPENDING TIME WITH OURSELVES

MK

What are some things individuals can do to improve their mental health on a personal level?

Carrie Tan

I think we don't spend enough time with ourselves, and what I mean is that we've gotten caught up and in a way, normalized ourselves to be busy and inundate ourselves and fill out our every single waking hour with something to do, that we forget to spend time with ourselves to listen to and nurture our own inner voice, which actually serves as our anchor and compass.

I remember when I was in my twenties, I was known to be a very outgoing person and even after work, every single week of the evening, I would line up something to take up my time, like dinner, a night out with friends, or something. There must be an activity. I wasn't comfortable with having a space of a couple of hours with nothing to do, and at some point I realized that hey, am I so uncomfortable with myself that I have to fill up every single waking hour with someone else's company, or some activity to distract myself? I realized that I'm running myself down being so busy doing all these activities. And although I'm having a lot of fun, why am I so afraid of spending time with myself? And then I made a deliberate effort to cut down my activities to make sure that every week, I have some space that I have not planned something for, to just have that window to spend time with myself. It's an ongoing endeavor.

[Carrie laughs]

Carrie Tan

Oftentimes that does not happen because now we have all these things to distract us. Most of the time it's work, but I think that it's a very precious and important practice in self-care to mark out regular windows of time in our calendar to spend time with ourselves.

MK

What were you looking for at that point in time?

Carrie Tan

Hmm. At that time, I wasn't sure what I was looking for but probably I was looking for my anchor and my compass but I didn't know it back then. I didn't have the language at that time to have such clarity about it. I just felt like you're drifting on in life, you're doing okay, you have a good job, you have friends and that seemed like normal life, right? But why do I always feel this unsettled feeling of restlessness, seeking for more fulfillment? And I didn't know where to look for this fulfillment and I just busied myself with the usual kind of activities that young people would fill up their time with lah.

So it wasn't until I went on a volunteer trip to India that it suddenly gave me something very specific to ponder about, which I pondered over for several years and that was the whole thing to do with gender discrimination, the plight of girls in India and my experience as a woman in Singapore. Thereafter, this became the main focus area of my life and my thoughts. Suddenly I had a problem that I was fixated about, and I really wanted to do something about it. Even though for several years I didn't know exactly what to do with this problem, it provided me with a lot of focus and I definitely felt less restless. In fact, it was very purposeful agitation inside myself where I had to kind of figure out exactly what I think is the right approach to tackle this issue that I care so much about.

MK

What are some interventions that as a collective, and even at a national level, that you think we should start implementing, if we want to improve the state of mental health in Singapore? Let me tell you the basis and premise of this question. With advancements in technology, the world is going to move at an even faster pace, and if we still remain disconnected from who we are as a person, at some level our mental health is going to get hit because mental health is related to who we are and our understanding of who we are as a person. It's going to snowball into other issues. So the thing is as an individual we talk about self-awareness, we talk about knowing ourselves but what can we do on a broader scale?

Carrie Tan

Well I think for a start, I'm taking a leaf out of the recent Earth Hour event right, where at this designated day and time, we're all going to switch off our lights for an hour. I think we can start with honouring our mental health in such a manner where we can have a dedicated day and time to do a mass collective sabbatical.

So that one day, we are encouraged to switch off from work, from busyness, and just to spend time with ourselves. I think that would be a good way to start signalling to society that this is important to us, nationally.

MK

Disconnect to connect.

Carrie Tan

Haha that's you doing a plug for ThisConnect. Yeah but pretty much like a World—I don't know if you can call it a World—Disconnect Day, but you know, take a break and honour yourself, honour time off for yourself. So I think if we can do that and have the support of the government to do that, I think that would be a huge milestone especially in modern society. I think a lot of what we do is driven by efficiency, productivity, etc. I think it'll be good if we can start off with a signal that rest is also as important.

MK

I think from this conversation what is coming up is that people tend to struggle with self-care, and by extension self-love.

Carrie Tan

I think it's a more common ailment or phenomenon than we realize. I think self-esteem issues are a major barrier to self-love and unfortunately, these self-esteem issues are often so subconscious and unconscious that people themselves may not be aware that they have self-esteem issues.

I mean, and it's not like, oh you see a dorky-looking person behaving awkwardly, and that's the face of someone with low self-esteem, right? I think it's an invisible problem because someone may come across and present themselves as very outgoing or confident, but could also actually have self-esteem issues. In fact, I think it's quite common knowledge that bullies tend to have self-esteem issues. So I think the level of self-awareness needs to be there to assess whether I really have self-esteem issues.

That was my own journey. I actually had self-esteem issues and I wondered where they came from. And when I traced it back I went back to my journey when I was a kid, and having parents who not knowingly, because they were parenting in a manner that they only knew how, but unwittingly caused some self-esteem issues. So I think it's on us as individuals to do the necessary self-work. For us to unpack that for ourselves and to make the necessary reconciliations with people in our lives who may have contributed to that. And to arrive at a state of okay, now I get why I felt that way and how do I affirm to myself that I am enough?

IT STARTS WITH BUILDING AWARENESS

MK

What's making people struggle with healing? We all know that it's important to heal ourselves, we all know that we need to love ourselves, don't we?
[laughs]

Carrie Tan

We don't all know that, Ming Kwang.

I think the mistake we make in life is that we assume that people know, but people don't know. Most of the time, we're just going about life. Even this language of the word 'healing' is not common at all outside of mental health circles, right? This notion of the fact that we need to heal ourselves, that we all have wounds, that we all have traumas, I mean even this lexicon is not common out of you, me, and the circles of people who pay attention to this. It's not common at all.

MK

'What trauma? I'm perfectly fine.'

Carrie Tan

Yeah, that's what is happening. So I think it's a lack of awareness that contributes to the stigmas and issues. Fundamentally a lack of awareness. And even with awareness, there is that fear of treading there to unpeel and uncover all these things because I mean, trauma in itself is a difficult experience. Why would you want to revisit that? I think what's common in the many cases that I've come across amongst friends, peers, people's stories is that typically people don't voluntarily go on that journey until something happens in their life that compels them to confront it. For me it was domestic violence and a marriage that just combusted, right? For others, it could be a serious illness, like having cancer. For others, it could be the loss of a job or some major crisis happening in their life that then propels them into this state where they really need to start figuring it out. Otherwise, I think they're kind of just cruising on in life. There isn't that strong compulsion to approach this as a form of necessary work.

MK

How can we advocate that?

Carrie Tan

Well, I think it starts with what you're doing which is collecting and sharing stories so that it becomes less uncommon. And I think having more stories like this may help to catalyse reflection in individuals and make them think about hey, do I relate to this, is this something that happened to me, is this why I started feeling a certain way after experiencing a certain thing? You know, so I think sharing more stories would help people to think more about themselves.

Because I mean this work of healing, it's not like people can come and do healing upon you. You kind of have to be self-motivated to reach out for external sources of support to give you the language, the tools, the frameworks to start understanding and navigating your own experiences. So I don't think we can impose it on people. I think it probably has to be ignited or catalysed through people sharing stories.

Perhaps one thing we can do as a society is to share and impart the skill of non-judgemental listening, because I think when we have conversations and people feel listened to, they're more likely to open up about their own experiences and in those conversations, they may then provide the opportunity for them to delve deeper into their own past or experiences to elicit introspection.

MK

If there's a message that you would like to tell the world about mental health, what would that be?

Carrie Tan

I think the work of knowing ourselves deeply and healing ourselves is the greatest work that we can do for ourselves and others. I believe that when we go through this journey and we do our self-work, it's likely that we will then be connected to our purpose and what we like to use the term 'calling'. More often than not in the individuals I've come across who have done this work, their purpose or their calling is in some way, some form or another, involved with service to others and service to humanity. I think if every individual sees it in our own personal responsibility as a human being on this earth to do that work for ourselves, the outcome of that would certainly bring positive contribution to society in some way or other.

CHAPTER FIFTEEN

It Takes a Whole Village

By Karen Wee, Deputy Executive Director, Lions Befrienders Service Association

The COVID-19 pandemic had a significant impact on the elderly, who could no longer visit community spaces such as the Lions Befrienders centre. When the centre opened after Circuit Breaker (CB),[12] Karen and her team had to work around social distancing restrictions as they interacted with the seniors. This episode is a testament that it takes a village to care for seniors, and that the community at large needs to come together to support our seniors.

---

[12] CB: Circuit Breaker refers to the three month nationwide lockdown in Singapore to curb the spread of COVID-19

EFFORTS TO SUPPORT THE ELDERLY IN THE POST-LOCKDOWN PERIOD

MK

Karen, thank you for making this work. I think the first question I want to ask you is about your personal experience in your job. During this CB period, domestic violence increased, and divorce rates also increased after lockdown commenced. There was also a case where a child actually took a knife and killed his father during a mental meltdown. Incidents like this one are happening within the whole social fabric of our country. What do you think is causing all these mental health issues to start surfacing?

Karen

Okay. So for us, we work with the elder care sector. 80 per cent of the seniors we serve stay in rental flats. It means that they stay alone, or in a tiny one-room flat day in day out. What's key to us is the fact that many have little or no education. Now, that means that technically, they're not like the rest of us who have access to technology. We are able to communicate with the outside world. For them, they're stuck. So that's one of the reasons why that's happening and how they're exhibiting it is of course, through attempted suicide. When they came out post-CB, there was disorientation, anxiety, and depression. They had meltdowns. One of them went to the doctor but forgot to bring his card and had a meltdown. He couldn't control his emotions, and we were called in to support him because we are the so-called equivalent to the next of kin.

Primarily for this group of seniors staying in rental flats, they have little or no education. Their normal way of survival is to use their hands and mouth to get by. When they want something, who is their greatest support? Their source of information is their peers. They can't read, so they're reliant on another human being for help. Again, during COVID, we still have connections, communication, we still watch the news, we still do Zooming, and we still talk. But for them, they have no access. It's not just about education. It's also the mindset. Because they didn't want to learn last time, they are afraid of learning now, and they're insecure. Anything you give them that's new, they will always tell you I've never studied, so you give me also I don't know how to use. So way before COVID a few years ago, AIC[13] distributed free smartphones to them. You'd typically be very happy to get free smartphones, right? You know what they did? There are a few outcomes, but basically no one is using it. One is they go and sell it to a *karang guni*[14]. They're very happy to get $10 for an $80 smartphone, because while it's brand new, it's of no use to them! They don't know how to use it. One of them is interesting, he wrapped it, and then kept it in the cabinet as if it was a precious gem.

So you can understand that even when you give them technology, they don't use it. Their mental health decline is quite severe. And what happened was that post-CB, we went into making sure that we have virtual befriending services at the SAC[15]. So LB[16] was one of the very few SSAs[17] who could reopen on day one of post-CB. We had all nine of our SACs 100 per cent open, approved for opening, by MOH[18] and AIC.

We know that seniors have issues. They fear using technology, but on the first day, we thought they'd be very excited to come down. And they did. We were at full capacity, but in the afternoon session, 40 per cent of the seats were empty. I was told that they finished the activity and had gone back already. But I said, after two months of being cooped up, aren't they happy to come out?

---

[13] AIC: Agency for Integrated Care

[14] Karang Guni: A Malay phrase that refers to men who collected unwanted items.

[15] SAC: Senior Activity Centre

[16] LB: Lions Befrienders

[17] SSA: Social Service Agency

[18] MOH: Ministry of Health

They said yeah, but they were task-driven, so they finished. The remaining 60 per cent, three out of five seniors, were shouting across the one-metre distance between the staff. They were there for social interaction. Then we realized that this was not sustainable. It was only day one, and we already had such situations. So what we did was to tell them okay, we realize that this is not sustainable in the long run, but I didn't have a solution then.

On day two, we had a meeting via Zoom, so I just asked them, 'Why don't we do this with seniors? Get them to Zoom'. The concern was because the seniors are not educated, they don't know how to use it. I said 'Never mind, let's use the opportunity to do something different'. So we managed to get ten seniors who were more open down to two centres, and got the centre managers to do it. They were above sixty years old and said let's try. But my HOD[19] was saying eh the last time we distributed handphones, our seniors already didn't want to do it. What makes you think they would want to go through this round? I said let's try lah!

When the seniors came, there was a world of difference. They sat through the entire sixty minutes. We had to sound so many alerts to ask them to leave because those were orders by MOH and AIC, we couldn't let them stay past sixty minutes. We had virtual volunteers who greeted them as they sat down at their stations, and they had conversations. Five to ten minutes after the ice breaker, we brought the screens out. We actually did share content, like playing games, and that's when the seniors started to panic. The staff were all on standby, so two staff had to run all over the place to make sure the screens were turned on and taught them. So we told the seniors 'No no no, now we got content, you can still see the person you're speaking with, the volunteer at the corner'.

Fast forward two months, when I went back to the site to check, there were seniors over eighty years old who couldn't read

---

[19] HOD: Head of Department

and write, but could play games on their own, like recognizing food and then matching it. For example, they could identify the word nasi lemak and match it with a picture of nasi lemak. And these were illiterates who could not read and write. They didn't even have smartphones. So they were able to handle it themselves perfectly on their own just two months into it. So this means, regarding mental health, when they actually have a friend and they're able to connect, they fare off much better.

Our fourth phase is to use AI technology pioneered and developed by ASTAR* researchers to identify the mental health of a person, for example, through facial recognition and body language. The Artificial Intelligence system appears as a clock with five-minute markings on our laptops. One hand indicates the level of happiness, and the other indicates the level of sadness. The nine o'clock hand represents sadness, ten o'clock represents depression, and eleven o'clock represents suicidal states. If the senior appears to be in a sad state for at least fifteen minutes, we send down a paracounsellor. If the senior appears to be in a depressive state for at least fifteen minutes, we assign a counsellor. If the senior appears to be in a suicidal state for at least fifteen minutes, we assign a psychiatrist.

So in terms of mental health decline, that's how we try to do early intervention, and what we're doing now is to make sure every staff is trained in and has a certification in mental health. Lions Befrienders is working on the holistic development of seniors' health. Social, emotional, mental, physical and spiritual health, all these aspects are important. We also sent our staff to the Yong Loo Lin School of Medicine to learn meditation, and this was all done since the second half of last year. Now, we are seeing the fruits of our labour. While we're ramping up, we also help them understand that dementia is going to hit one in ten seniors, so all our centres are now dementia to-go zones and we're very much moving into dementia and early prevention in mental health. Okay, over to you, next question!

DON'T SAY I DON'T KNOW

MK

Got it, Karen. I think your answer covers a lot of interesting domains and it's very powerful. I'm wondering . . . To implement all these things, it's going to take a while. What can communities and individuals start doing first, as a support system or even as an intervention, to hold themselves to a certain awareness in terms of what they're really dealing with, so that they can find an easier way to look for answers if it's necessary? Rather than allow things to drag on. Because I do notice that if we're talking about the previous generation, there is a lack of understanding, so a person might not even know that they're depressed until further down the road when things start spiraling down.

Karen

What we need are multiple efforts. One, you need the community to be aware, to know what to do and to identify early signs. There are places known as dementia-friendly zones. So in some parts of Singapore, they actually have the community already ready. Shopkeepers are trained to identify a senior with dementia if they get lost. They know to bring them to the dementia to-go point. That is what the community can do.

Secondly, mental health is several-pronged. One is mental wellness, another one is mental illness. So the thing you must understand is that we are looking at mental wellness. The community can only do early detection of mental health issues. Every one of us is responsible for our own mental wellness. What is needed in maintaining our mental wellness is for the seniors themselves to be aware. We try to explain and encourage them to observe for themselves, but sometimes, they can't see. Usually, they don't have friends, so we befriend them, and our staff are able to see the decline. Now, what you want the community volunteers to do is also to be an advocate. Dementia has a free range. You need to know that once you have early signs, you need to seek activities to correct it. Dementia is basically like an onion. The core of it is their youth, their earlier days. Usually the inner core, the bulk of the onion, is protected. But the outer layers are affected, and the degree to which they are affected will put the seniors in different stages. Either early-stage dementia, moderate stage, or advanced stage dementia. Now, when it comes to high-moderate dementia, the person is usually gone already, you can't reverse it they have already lost most of their cognition. So whatever you do, dementia is irreversible. You can only slow it down that's the challenge. So when we formulate our approaches, we must make sure that if we're dealing with, let's say, a case of high-moderate dementia, you definitely have to bring them into dementia daycare already, you have to. Unless you have a lot of caregivers to handle it.

So the issue is, your caregiver might also be stressed. It's not easy, because day and night are all reversed. You can't even sleep at night as a caregiver. So to help yourself, you have to—this is my suggestion—have a support network either for yourself, or most importantly, for the person with dementia. It's actually in their best interest to go to a daycare because we have medical teams there and it gives you a break. You need that. It's not about abandoning your family members if you put them in a daycare. It's a daycare, you still bring them home at night! So we have exercises there to tire them out and make sure they don't decline further. It's actually in our interest to make sure we intervene at that point in time to slow down the decline, because that's all we can do. But in early-moderate and early stages, it's very important to also give them appropriate activities so that you stop the early-stage decline and the person remains aware. So certain activities will help certain parts of the brain function, and that's important. What we need is advocacy, so that the general public and the community knows what dementia is, and so that they have a proper understanding and can identify people around them whether it's their neighbour or their grandparents. Don't say I don't know. Because what happens is that the earlier you identify this, the better it is in your interest. You help the whole community.

CHAPTER SIXTEEN

Holding the Hope

By Tina Huang, Senior Consultant, National Council of Social Service

There are many facets to mental health, and everyone experiences it in their own unique ways. Unlike going to a doctor for physical illness, mental health treatment needs different social services to collaborate and integrate with one another such that the support and individual receives address their issues holistically. More importantly, Tina highlights that we have to fight shame and stigma with love and courage to support people on their recovery journey.

DEVELOPING THE MENTAL HEALTH LANDSCAPE THROUGH THE YEARS

MK

Could you share with us about the work that you do in NCSS[20]? What made you decide to go into this profession? What led you to make a very strong stand for the mental health cause?

Tina

For many years, I looked after the services and fund allocation issues in the social service sector. In other words, I'm always looking at how the whole sector can deliver better services and where the gaps are. From time to time, we would look at piloting solutions to bridge the gaps identified. NCSS also mobilizes resources, conducts fundraising, and builds capabilities.

In 2014, I set up a mental health services team inside NCSS because I noticed this emerging need and thought more could be done. And if we look at what worked for other countries, we would be able to learn quickly and pick up tested ideas more quickly. I began consulting local leaders, including those in IMH, and I also met some leaders from the US who are themselves persons in recovery, who have created a lot of programmes, services, and initiatives that they tell me have worked very well for many decades in America, and have touched tens of thousands of lives of people with mental health conditions. In 2015, I brought a group of leaders from social service agencies to look at what the Americans were doing and to bring some of those ideas back to help us break new grounds. That's how the Peer Support Specialist Programme was created. We also created Beyond the Label,[21] the public education movement, and we

---

[20] NCSS: National Council of Social Service

[21] Beyond the Label: http://facebook.com/beyondthelabelsg

then set up Resilience Collective under the Caregivers Alliance and Binjaitree.

In the same year, NCSS embarked on the Quality of Life Study for vulnerable populations which sparked a lot more initiatives and conversations, and people started looking at services differently. We went and asked people what do you need? How is your quality of life? What do you want to improve? We also realized very quickly that while persons in recovery may have a certain view, the rest of society has a different view of them. We conducted a Study on Public Attitudes towards Persons with Mental Health Conditions in 2017. We asked Singaporeans aged eighteen to fifty-nine years old several questions about how they see people with mental health conditions. Would they live near them? Would they befriend them? Would they give them jobs if they are employers? With the results, I thought we needed to do something about stigma. It was in the way of people getting help, getting jobs, and being able to fulfil their potential. That's how the Beyond the Label campaign came into being.

A LACK OF UNDERSTANDING LEADS TO AVOIDANCE AND STIGMA

MK

What are some of the mental health stigmas you've observed, being on the ground for so long over the last few years?

Tina

I've met with different groups of people with mental health conditions and listened to the struggles they face. There were young adults and not so young adults people who have finished school, in the workplace, in the marketplace. The stories that they were telling me contained a lot of stereotypes about who they were perceived to be, or who they became, as soon as there was a diagnosis. These very bright and talented people were suddenly perceived as not going to be able to work, as people who shouldn't be given responsibilities, and so on. This caused a lot of hardship and pain in their lives in terms of getting and keeping a job. In fact, they used to tell me Tina, we can't tell anybody we have a condition. We will never get an interview.

But I must say that while it's true that some parts of our society still practice discriminatory behaviour, we are making progress. We are shifting. COVID, interestingly, has helped to bring this conversation into the public space. While some segments of society continue to have this sort of stereotypical thinking, I encourage people in recovery to disclose, and I will share why.

What they told me was, when they don't disclose, they take their medication, go back for treatment, and review in secret. When they need to take time off to either go to the hospital or have some respite, they cannot tell the truth. And this causes their employer to say you don't seem to be very interested in this job. Do you really want to work? After a while, they either resign or they've been told we don't need you here because you're taking so much time off and you can't tell us why. If you disclose, you can then have this conversation with your employer about the kind of support you need. You can be truthful about seeking treatment. If they're supportive of you, it's a good place for you and you should thrive. If they're not supportive, perhaps that is not a friendly environment for you to be in, in the first place. I feel that people with mental health conditions should not give away all their power. They, too, should have a choice and decide. While there's some amount of external stigma from society, there is also self-stigma stemming from shame and cultural taboos. Sometimes, they choose not to seek treatment until someone tells them we know someone you can go and seek help from, who has helped me, and it has worked for other people as well. They need encouragement. The self-stigma is very real because they put themselves in a place that is lower than they need to be, and that gets in the way of their contributing and living their potential.

MK

What are the transformations in society you think we can expect, moving forward? We see these stigmas now. But ten years ago, this conversation wouldn't even exist, true?

Tina

Absolutely.

MK

[laughing] That's why you set up Resilience Collective and Beyond the Label!

Tina

I feel very blessed that I can do a small part to try and normalize these conversations. To answer your question, I want to share a book. [Tina holds up the book]

MK

Let me write that down. Speaking Up for Mental Illness . . . Wow!

Tina

Professor Kua Ee Heok went to prestigious schools like Oxford and Harvard. So when this very promising medical doctor chose to be a psychiatrist and went to work at IMH, he wrote this book and shared how his neighbours and relatives laughed at him. A lot of people felt sorry for him. In those days, IMH was called Woodbridge Hospital, so they said oh my goodness, you're going to Woodbridge Hospital. Why would you do that? But he persevered and went to work there.

So, sharing that fear and misconception about people with mental health conditions, and the mental health condition itself, leads to the next reaction, avoidance. People tend to avoid what they don't understand, whether it's a person at work, in the community, relatives, or whoever. Avoidance. The other reaction is social exclusion. Intentionally or unintentionally, there is social exclusion going on in our society. And when we interviewed persons with mental health conditions for the Quality of Life Study, they told us that they really want to be socially included. After we did the analysis, we discovered that the key is social inclusion. If we do just this one thing as a society, it will help give them hope in almost every area of their life. These are some things we need to get on with, do better, and rise higher in.

REASONS PEOPLE DO NOT SEEK HELP

MK

Let's look at it from an individual point of view. What do you think is preventing people from seeking help?

Tina

The Singapore Mental Health Study conducted by IMH in 2016 cited past research which found two major reasons why people are not seeking help. The first is that they may not recognize the symptoms. They may not know that they are going through something that is more serious, something that requires a diagnosis and proper treatment. On that note, I want to tell you about this book—
[Tina holds up the book]

MK

A Philosopher's Madness by Li Shan Chan . . .

Tina

Li Shan used to be my staff. She wrote this book before I met her. In the book, she described the heartbreaking, very honest journey of how she discovered that she had schizophrenia. And she didn't know she had this condition. She started to talk to herself, climbed out of her ledge, and was fired by her employer. She was arrested because she was talking to herself in a public place. This book is a very honest, insightful book about her journey. It is just one person's journey, but I suspect it's more common than we know. When she realized that she had a mental health condition that required treatment, she went to IMH. Another person I have spoken with was Jeremy, who told me Tina, I didn't even know I had depression after my mother died. He was her caregiver. He didn't know until his pastor said Jeremy, I think this is something quite serious. It's really affecting you. It's gone on for a few months. I think you should seek help. Only then did he start on his recovery journey. It took him about four years to recover with medication and therapy. When he recovered, he wanted to use his lived experience to help others in their recovery journey. He attended NCSS' training to attain the Certificate for Peer Support Specialist. Today, he is a champion for seeking help early and helping to fight the stigma.

The second reason cited in the 2016 IMH study on why people don't seek help is stigma. Plain and simple. If people are going to think less of me, if it's going to get in the way of my functioning fully in society, then perhaps I'm not going to say anything. I'm not going to go and seek help because I will have this negative label that I have a mental health condition. Not only will I be affected, my loved ones and friends will also be affected.

MK

Got it.
[short pause]

MK

Anything else you want to add on to that?

Tina

COVID has changed the equation, right? I feel sad that more Singaporeans are experiencing mental health challenges. There is a rise in reported cases of people requiring help, wanting counselling, experiencing more anxieties, and fearing the unknown because COVID means that they might lose their jobs, because businesses are not doing well. There's this confluence of factors.

As a society, as a country, we need to learn how to build resilience among our general population, not just a small group of people. How do we get people to a better place so that they not only can cope, but they can thrive? For the smaller group of people who require treatment, we want them to seek treatment early. I have discovered how important this is. With COVID, kids are spending more time not in school, but at home. Sometimes we get on each other's nerves. I want to make a special appeal to parents to look out for signs that their children may not be doing so well. Maybe they are going through some anxieties or going through a difficult period. We all need to listen more, and judge less. As parents, we need to learn more ways of supporting our children, there are a lot of seminars, webinars, and information posted on the web, on social media. You just need to do a search. There are also many parenting groups. In fact, if I can just mention a few.

The PleaseStay Movement was launched by parents in 2019. These parents have lost a child to suicide, and they've decided to turn their pain into something positive that helps other parents, other families, and other youths. There are trends out there that are very negative for young people, and they can get information on how to commit suicide online. It's very scary for parents. Another non-profit organization started by parents is Over the Rainbow. Yen-Lu lost his son to depression and wants to reach out to help others, as many as possible. Linda Collins, a great writer, wrote a beautiful and heartbreaking book, Lost Adjustment, about the death and suicide of her daughter. There's a lot of information out there. I think we all need to be curious and learn, because we can't care about something we don't understand. We need to go and understand our children, our young people, so that we can figure out how to support them. There are also many social service agencies serving in this area. You can check out the Mental Health Resource Directory[22] in the NCSS website. I mentioned Resilience Collective. Club HEAL supports Malay Muslims who have mental health conditions. The Singapore Mental Health Film Festival is for people who enjoy watching films and is another source of insightful information that uses art to communicate. The government, through agencies across sectors like healthcare, social, education and employment, are coming together to try and take a more holistic approach to tackle this issue and I think that is the correct approach. We must work together. I said that in the beginning too, we need to have less boundaries, less lines and work more seamlessly when it comes to mental wellness and mental illness.

SERVICE INTEGRATION TO ENABLE FASTER AND SAFE ACCESS TO HELP

MK

COVID has turned a lot of things around, which means that when we look at mental health, we can no longer look at it from the old factors we are used to. We need to have more consideration of the new factors that are in play right now, in our time, in our existing circumstances. I'm just wondering, what are some interventions we can look forward to?

Tina

I think society has traditionally worked in separate spheres. People who are sick go to the hospital, see the doctors, nurses, and they discharge and go home. That's the end of it.

But I think for something like mental wellness and mental health conditions, the healthcare sector, both hospitals and agencies,

---

[22] Mental Health Resource Directory: go.gov.sg/ncss-mentalhealthresources

must work very closely and seamlessly with the community and the social service sector. There must be this handshake so that people are not lost. Currently, if they have a crisis, whether it's suicide or a psychosis breakdown, they will go to the hospital, then they go home, and we wouldn't know where they are. Or, they're out in the community and not seeking the treatment that they need. Going forward, we all need to work more seamlessly together. The professionals who work in these two sectors need to get together and have this exchange of perspectives, views, and ideas on what they can do differently and better so that the service users are better. The other idea is what's beyond formal structured services like funding, day centres, counselling services, and so on. Yes, we need all that. We need to, in fact, grow the depth of our expertise in those areas. But we also need to get the information to youths and adults who need to access these services.

MK

That's what I thought too. That's why I started ThisConnect. I realized that we needed to start rallying different mental health professionals and groups to come together. Because everybody is doing their own thing. Sometimes if we come together collectively as an intention, then the effect and impact is larger.

GETTING HELP

Tina

Yes. Many people have asked me Tina, I have a neighbour or friend or church friend who needs to seek help. Where can that person go to get help? I get a lot of these queries. That means people still don't know where to go to seek help. So that's one, the access issue that we need to tackle. Of course, in terms of cost, it needs to be affordable. We must be in different spaces depending on the service user's profile. Does the way we organize ourselves let them know where to find help? The way we deliver our services needs to consider their ability to access those services. By making services much more accessible, I hope this will take away the stigma that only people who are terribly sick must go to IMH. No. We should be able to seek help and not be worried about being judged. It's not unlike breaking a bone or something physical and going to a doctor. We need to normalize the help-seeking behaviour and the recovery journey. I think we don't speak enough about recovery. We're always focused on mental illnesses and how people can't do things. We need to focus more on the fact that people, with the help and support from their immediate support system of family and friends, can get better. They recover. They can work.

I was at the Youth Mental Wellbeing Network that MSF,[23] MOH[24] and MOE[25] jointly lead. I told them if you don't know where to go look for support and help, go to the mental health directory on the NCSS website. There's also a help bot called Belle,[26] for young people, especially. It's interactive, anonymous, and it will point people in the right direction based on what they are telling Belle. We've listed other helplines and resources as well. There is one more thing I want to say.

[Tina holds up a book]

PEOPLE WITH LIVED EXPERIENCE CAN PLAY CRITICAL ROLES IN RECOVERY

MK

Holding the Hope . . .

---

[23] MSF: Ministry of Social and Family Development

[24] MOH: Ministry of Health

[25] MOE: Ministry of Education

[26] Belle helpbot: https://go.gov.sg/belle-helpbot

Tina

When we created the Peer Support Specialist Programme to train people who have mental health conditions, we trained them on their own recovery plan and to stay on recovery. The peer support specialists are trained and certified, and they want to use their lived experience to help somebody else on their recovery journey.

MK

Paying it forward.

Tina

IMH has hired peer support specialists to complement their doctors and nurses. They function like case workers and assistants. Some of our social service agencies have hired them to also do counselling and make home visits, to journey with people who are in recovery. They are very powerful because they've lived through a condition themselves, whatever the condition may be, and they've arrived at a point where they are speaking up about their mental health condition. Beyond seeking help and recovering, they also want to help other people recover. NCSS has trained ninety-eight peer support specialists. This is a book that they have put together to tell the world about what they have lived through and how they got to the point that they are at today. Many different stories because mental illness affects people from all walks of lives.

Every year when I attend their graduation, they tell their stories. It's very emotional and very inspiring. We invite their families and network to support them and to hear their very personal and life changing stories.

Beyond the Label would never have taken off without them. It took off because the people who have a condition started to join us and started to tell their stories. And I know how hard it is, how brave they are to be able to do that. So, I think I got more out of this process of trying to give, because I learned so much about courage and about love. These guys are the heroes. All our ambassadors are heroes.

FIGHT SHAME AND STIGMA WITH LOVE AND COURAGE

Tina

Do you have any burning questions?

MK

I think the final burning question would be this: if you were to send out a message about mental health to the public, whether it is in our local context or even internationally, what would that be for you?

Tina

I would say, fight shame and stigma with love and courage. And I know the word shame is very uncomfortable. It makes everybody immediately very uncomfortable. Yet, if we don't name things we need to confront, if we always go around the bush and never confront it, change cannot happen. I think when we say the name—in this case, shame, and stigma—we begin the journey of overcoming it. And when I meet others who are experts, who have spent their whole lives researching or providing services in this area, they tell me the same thing. There's a lot of fear, shame, and stigma, and that gets in the way of people getting on the recovery journey. We all must do our part. So that will be my parting shot.

MK

Got it. Thank you for that.

The path to finding the answers is not easy by any means, and sometimes the answers aren't what we expect them to be. But there are 1,001 reasons not to do something, and you only need one to do it—because **your life matters**. Doors and windows of opportunity open when they do, and it is up to you to step in. If the experience of this book has sparked something deeper in you that you wish to examine, let this be another sign from the universe to keep going.

If you'd like to reach out to have a conversation with us, our doors are open.

Send us a message on Instagram at **@thisconnect.today,** and we'll be happy to connect with you.

Bibliography

Manpower Research & Statistics Department, Ministry of Manpower, "Long-Term Unemployment Rate and Number Concepts and Definitions." https://stats.mom.gov.sg/SL/Pages/Long-Term-Unemployment-Level-and-Rate-Concepts-and-Definitions.aspx.

Subramaniam, M., E. Abdin, J. A. Vaingankar, S. Shafie, B. Y. Chua, R. Sambasivam, Y. J. Zhang, et al., "Tracking the Mental Health of a Nation: Prevalence and Correlates of Mental Disorders in the Second Singapore Mental Health Study." *Epidemiology and Psychiatric Sciences* 29, 2020: e29. doi:10.1017/S2045796019000179.

Acknowledgements

I would like to express our heartfelt gratitude to all the people who have played a part in making this book come to life. To our contributors, thank you for jumping in and contributing your time, energy, and intention towards forwarding the mental health scene in Singapore. It is a work in progress, and perhaps it may take more than just one lifetime to see the transformation unfold, yet your desire to make a difference to the people out there is instrumental to keeping the vision alive for our future generations, in wellness and prosperity. I am grateful to all of you for the good work that is being done out there and I look forward to more efficient and effective interventions to touch the lives out there.

To the people working with me in the background, Si Qi and Megan, I want to thank you for supporting me in facilitating the process so that these interviews and the backend work could happen. Your beliefs in the cause and my vision, your stand, dedication, and devotion in the project have inspired me to keep going, to push forth to produce a higher quality of work that is nothing less than being impeccable and excellent. This book would not have been completed without your support and commitment.

We embarked on this project with the simple objective to document the different perspectives around mental health in Singapore, yet we walked out of each interview session feeling deeply inspired by selfless acts of service from all these contributors.

These interview sessions have shaped our understanding of what service to the community means, no matter big or small, and we deeply cherish the life lessons and personal takeaways we received from all the contributors.

I would also like to attribute and honor all my masters and teachers for being my greatest sources of inspiration for my work, and the trust and faith they placed in me in carrying the work forward to make a difference in this world; trusting in me to do the right thing and getting my act together during my lowest point and being there with me to celebrate my successes and endeavors during my highest peaks. Without them, I would not have been the person I am today. Every single day, I wake up looking forward to live my mark with love, passion and joy.

Finally, I would like to conclude with a quote from Thoreau, Henry David Thoreau, Walden, or Life in the Woods:

"I went to the woods because I wished to live deliberately, to front only the essential facts of life, and see if I could not learn what it had to teach, and not, when I came to die, discover that I had not lived. I did not wish to live what was not life, living is so dear; nor did I wish to practice resignation, unless it was quite necessary. I wanted to live deep and suck out all the marrow of life, to live so sturdily and Spartan-like as to put to rout all that was not life, to cut a broad swath and shave close, to drive life into a corner, and reduce it to its lowest terms, and, if it proved to be mean, why then to get the whole and genuine meanness of it, and publish its meanness to the world; or if it were sublime, to know it by experience, and be able to give a true account of it in my next excursion."

This is an experience we will remember for a lifetime, and we hope that it has inspired you to continue doing the work that you do too. This is only the beginning, and there is so much more to learn, many more steps to take, and much more work to be done. We hope to honour all our contributors by doing our part to champion mental health causes so that we can create an inclusive, thriving society where people are deeply connected to themselves, to the present, and to the world around them. Thank you.

Acknowledgements

Adrian Pang
Pangdemonium

Amirah Munawwarah
ImPossible
Psychological Services

Andrea Chan
Joel Wong
Lucia Chow
Peggy Lim
TOUCH Community
Services Ltd

Asher Low
Limitless

Belinda Ang
ARTO by thinkART of the
Box Pte Ltd

Brenda Lee
Lynn Tan
The Psychology Practice

Buvenasvari Pragasam
Solace Art
Psychotherapy Pte Ltd

Camellia Wong
InPsychful LLP

Carrie Tan
Nee Soon South
(Nee Soon GRC)

Calvin Eng
Association for Music
Therapy (Singapore)

Charlotte Goh
Playeum

Cheryl Chan
Fengshan (East Coast GRC)

Cayden Woo
Jeremy Heng
Singapore
Children's Society

243

Cho Ming Xiu
Campus PSY Limited

Daphne Chua
Somatic Therapy Asia

David Chew
National Heritage Board

David Lim
Tzu Chi Free Clinic
Special Oral Care Network
Deborah Seah
Nadera Binte Abdul Aziz
Community of Peer Support
Specialists (CPSS)

Desmond Chew
Jacqueline
Jamie
Mysara
Caregivers Alliance Limited

Desmond Soh
Annabelle Psychology

Eric Chua
Ministry of Culture,
Community and Youth
Ministry of Social and
Family Development

Etsegenet Mulugeta Eshete
Margaret Hoffer
Selamta Family Project

Goh Li Shan
REACH (West)
Department of
Psychological Medicine,
National
University Hospital

Hannah Batrisyia
Muhammad Syazan Bin Saad
Temasek Polytechnic

Jamus Lim
Anchorvale
(Sengkang GRC)

Jasmine Yeo
The Private Practice

Jenny Ng
Conscious Parenting Coach
(MEd of Family Education)

Jingzhou
Cassia Resettlement Team

Josephine Chia-Teo
InSightful Training &
Consultancy Pte Ltd

John Wong Chee Meng
**Department of
Psychological Medicine,
National
University Hospital**

Jun Lee
**Self-employed Art Therapist
and Art Facilitator**

Karen Wee
**Lions Befrienders Service
Association**

Kyl Lim
Singapore Cancer Society

Lynette Har
**ICF-Certified Peak
Performance Coach**

Lynette Seow
Safe Space™

Marion Neubronner
**Psychologist
and Leadership
Development Coach**

Michelle Koay
**St. Joseph's Institution
International Ltd**

Murali Pillai
Bukit Batok SMC

Narasimman S/O
Tivasiha Mani
Impart Ltd

Navin Amarasuriya
**The Contentment
Foundation**

Natalie Kang
**Art for Good Pte Ltd
MySpace Psychotherapy
Services Pte Ltd**

Nicole K.
The Tapestry Project SG

Jolene
**Volunteer in the Migrant
Worker Space**

Nur Farhan Bte
Mohammad Alami
Raffles Medical Group

Ng Gim Choo
The EtonHouse Group

Ng Jek Mui
Dementia Singapore

(formerly known as
**Alzheimer's Disease
Association)**

Patrick Tay
Pioneer SMC

Rachel Yang
Daylight Creative Therapies

Ronald P.M.H. Lay
**LASALLE College
of the Arts**

Roshni Bhatia
Yoko Choi
FoundSpace

Seah Kian Peng
**Braddell Heights (Marine
Parade GRC)**

Serene Seng
Senserene Pte Ltd

Siew Kum Yew
**Shan You
Counselling Centre**

Simone Heng
Human Connection Speaker

Sun Kaiying
**Hope for Tomorrow
Psychology Centre**

Sufian Yusof
Aileron Wellness

Tina Hung
**National Council of Social
Service (NCSS)**

Tin Pei Ling
MacPherson SMC
Wan Rizal Bin Wan Zakariah
**Kolam Ayer (Jalan
Besar GRC)**

Vickineswarie Jagadharan
OTHERS

Victor Mills
Michael Chang
Sujata Tiwari
**Singapore International
Chamber of Commerce**

Ying Jie

About THISCONNECT.TODAY

THIS
. CON
NECT

ThisConnect is a mental health advocacy community set up to spark more conscious awareness and forwarding interventions on mental health, emotional wellness, and suicide prevention using experiential art. We recognise the need to begin the mental health conversations by examining the personal struggles that weigh us down in life. These everyday stressors can seem insignificant on their own, but over a long period of time, they can make us feel trapped, lost, stressed, and depressed. Through our work, we want to inspire more people to step out, to connect consciously and deeply with themselves physically, emotionally, mentally and spiritually, and to find the healing with the good and the bad, the positive and the negative, the light and the shadow within them. We want people to access their courage, love, freedom in their beings to express their most authentic selves, and to create a life where they are thriving. We hope that our work will empower individuals to seek help and to look inwards whenever they face challenges in life.

Since 2020, we have presented three large multimedia art exhibitions and thirteen moving satellite shows in Singapore, titled *ThisConnect: Threading Worlds*, Masks of Singapore, and *ThisConnect: What Am I, If I Am Not*, and were featured in *The Straits Times*,

Tatler, Channel 8. Masks of Singapore, a six-month community participatory art project movement, has set the record for the 'Largest Mosaic of Hand-Sculptured Masks' in the Singapore Book of Records and were documented into a photobook with Fujifilm that tells 572 lived-stories of individuals from all walks of lives in their most authentic self behind the masks created.

For more information, reach out at

ThisConnect.today@gmail.com.
https://www.thisconnect.today
https://www.instagram.com/thisconnect.today

'Oftentimes, external expectations about who we should be and how we should act prevent us from being free to express ourselves and do the things that truly matter to us. As a result, many of us end up chasing after societal definitions of success instead of what truly matters to us, and we end up lost, confused, and disconnected from ourselves. It is this disconnection from ourselves that forms the start of the many mental and emotional struggles we face every day, and it is potentially leads to depression, and on a more severe scale, suicide. Through our work, we aim to explore the deeper conversations that underpin the mental health struggles many of us battle in our daily lives and empower people to connect to themselves, to the present, and the world around them. Ultimately, the goal is to see a society where people are free to be bold, be free, and be themselves—unapologetically—so that they can begin to live a life that matters to them.'

Hun Ming Kwang,
Founder, Creative Director,
Author of ThisConnect.today